COFFEE WITH CARL ROGERS

Conversations on Empathy, Growth, and Personal Transformation

Take the 10-Day
LEADERSHIP TRANSFORMATION CHALLENGE:
Unlock Your Potential!

** A Challenge for Transformation:*

Commit to reading for a minimum of 10 days and fearlessly attempt all self-assessment activities to emerge as a profoundly transformed leader*

MEERA KHANNA

INDIA · SINGAPORE · MALAYSIA

Copyright © Meera Khanna 2023
All Rights Reserved.

ISBN 979-8-89066-814-1

This book has been published with all efforts taken to make the material error-free after the consent of the author. However, the author and the publisher do not assume and hereby disclaim any liability to any party for any loss, damage, or disruption caused by errors or omissions, whether such errors or omissions result from negligence, accident, or any other cause.

While every effort has been made to avoid any mistake or omission, this publication is being sold on the condition and understanding that neither the author nor the publishers or printers would be liable in any manner to any person by reason of any mistake or omission in this publication or for any action taken or omitted to be taken or advice rendered or accepted on the basis of this work. For any defect in printing or binding the publishers will be liable only to replace the defective copy by another copy of this work then available.

Your Support Makes a Difference!

By embarking on this transformative journey through "A Challenge for Transformation: Coffee with Carl Rogers," not only will you be enriching your own leadership skills, but you will also be making a difference in the lives of orphaned, poor, and needy children.

It is with great joy that Meera Khanna announces that **100%** of the proceeds from this book will be donated to an NGO dedicated to supporting these children. If you're interested in learning more about the NGO and how you can contribute, please reach out to the author directly at hello@meerakhanna.com

Together, let's create a better future for those who need it most.

TABLE OF CONTENTS

SECTION 1: ABOUT THE AUTHOR

Meera Khanna, the author of "Coffee with Carl Rogers: Conversations on Empathy, Growth, and Personal Transformation," is a visionary leader and passionate advocate for empathetic leadership. With a wealth of experience in organizational development and a deep understanding of the human dynamics within teams, Meera brings a unique perspective to the realm of leadership and personal growth.

As an accomplished professional and thought leader, Meera Khanna has dedicated her career to helping individuals and organizations thrive through the power of empathy. With a background in psychology and extensive expertise in leadership development, Meera has made it her mission to integrate the principles of empathy, personal transformation, and growth into the fabric of modern workplaces.

Meera's journey has been shaped by her deep appreciation for the groundbreaking work of Carl Rogers, the renowned psychologist known for his humanistic approach and emphasis on empathy. Inspired by Rogers' teachings, Meera sought to create a practical guide that bridges the gap between theory and application, empowering leaders to cultivate empathy and create transformative workplace cultures.

Through her book, "Coffee with Carl Rogers," Meera seamlessly weaves together insightful dialogues, actionable concepts, and reflective exercises to provide a comprehensive roadmap for empathetic leadership. By drawing on her own experiences and expertise, she offers a fresh and engaging perspective on how empathy can be harnessed as a catalyst for personal and professional growth.

Through her work, Meera Khanna seeks to inspire leaders to embrace empathy as a powerful tool for transformation and to create environments that prioritize human connection and personal development. With her deep understanding of organizational dynamics and her commitment to driving meaningful change, Meera continues to shape the conversation around empathetic leadership and pave the way for a more compassionate and growth-oriented future.

Join Meera Khanna on this transformative journey as she invites you to discover the profound impact that empathy can have on your leadership style, your teams, and your organization as a whole. Through "Coffee with Carl Rogers," Meera empowers leaders to embark on a path of personal and professional growth, unlocking their true potential while fostering environments that thrive on empathy, understanding, and collaboration.

13

Section 2: Introduction

Welcome to "Coffee with Carl Rogers: Conversations on Empathy, Growth, and Personal Transformation." In this book, we embark on a journey to explore the transformative power of empathy and its profound impact on personal and professional growth. In this book, we draw upon Rogers' teachings to explore how empathy can be integrated into leadership practices. We leverage his profound understanding of human nature and interpersonal dynamics to offer practical guidance and actionable strategies for leaders who aspire to create transformative workplace cultures.

Empathy, the ability to understand and share the feelings of another, is a critical skill that fosters connection, collaboration, and positive change. It is the cornerstone of effective leadership, creating an environment where individuals feel seen, heard, and valued. By cultivating empathy, leaders can inspire their teams, promote personal growth, and drive meaningful transformations within their organizations.

But first, let's meet Carl Rogers—the influential psychologist who serves as our guide in this exploration. Carl Rogers was a renowned figure in the field of humanistic psychology. He dedicated his life to studying and promoting the importance of empathy, unconditional positive regard, and authenticity in human relationships. Rogers believed that empathy—the ability to understand and share the feelings of another—played a pivotal role in fostering growth, self-actualization, and personal transformation.

Each chapter of this book focuses on a specific concept related to empathy, growth, and personal transformation. We begin by introducing a concept, such as active listening, psychological safety, emotional intelligence, unconditional positive regard (UPR), or vulnerability, among others. These concepts serve as building blocks for developing empathetic leadership skills.

Following the introduction of each concept, we present a dialogue between an employee and a leader. Through these dialogues, we bring the concepts to life, demonstrating how they can be applied in real-world scenarios. The dialogues provide practical examples of how empathy can be expressed, understood, and embraced within the dynamics of employee-leader relationships.

After each dialogue, we explore the outcomes and implications of applying the concept. We delve into the positive impact that empathy can have on trust, communication, collaboration, and personal growth. By understanding the potential outcomes, leaders can better grasp the significance of incorporating empathy into their leadership practices.

To facilitate practical application, we provide a blank section after each demonstration where leaders can reflect on their current scenarios. This section acts as a personal space for leaders to identify areas for improvement, take note of specific challenges they face, and strategize how they can apply the concepts discussed to their unique situations. It encourages leaders to take an introspective approach, fostering self-awareness and the development of empathetic leadership skills.

Through the dialogues, concepts, and reflection sections, "Coffee with Carl Rogers" aims to empower leaders to embrace empathy as a catalyst for growth, transformation, and enhanced interpersonal relationships. It invites leaders to go beyond traditional approaches, fostering a culture of empathy, understanding, and personal development within their teams and organizations.

By having a virtual "coffee" with Carl Rogers, we pay tribute to his groundbreaking work and aim to continue his legacy in bringing empathy to the forefront of leadership and personal development. Through these imagined conversations, we strive to channel Rogers' wisdom and insights, intertwining them with practical scenarios to provide valuable guidance for leaders seeking to create empathetic and growth-oriented environments.

By engaging in "Coffee with Carl Rogers," we invite leaders to reflect on their own leadership styles, challenge traditional approaches, and embrace empathy as a powerful tool for personal and collective advancement.

So, grab a virtual cup of coffee and join us on this journey of self-discovery, as we tap into the wisdom of Carl Rogers and explore the transformative potential of empathy in our quest for personal and professional growth. Together, let's have a conversation that nurtures empathy, sparks insights, and paves the way for meaningful transformation.

SECTION 3: (Dis)CLAIMER

In this book, we embark on a transformative journey to explore the power of empathy and its profound impact on leadership and personal growth. Each chapter is designed to engage and challenge you, providing valuable insights, practical strategies, and thought-provoking self-assessment activities.

At the end of each chapter, you will find a self-assessment activity tailored to the concepts and principles discussed. These activities are intended to encourage introspection, reflection, and personal growth. They serve as powerful tools for you to evaluate your current practices, beliefs, and behaviors, allowing you to identify areas for improvement and chart a path towards becoming a more empathetic and effective leader.

We make a strong claim and promise: If you commit to reading this book for a minimum of 10 days, dedicating yourself to each chapter and diligently attempting all self-assessment activities, you will emerge as a changed leader. This book is designed to be more than just a collection of ideas and theories; it is a roadmap for personal transformation and leadership growth.

Through the combination of rich dialogue, practical examples, and interactive self-assessment activities, you will have the opportunity to deepen your understanding, challenge your perspectives, and apply newfound knowledge to your leadership approach. By engaging in these activities, you will develop the skills and mindset necessary to create empathetic connections, foster growth within your team, and drive positive change in your organization.

We invite you to fully immerse yourself in the journey presented within these pages. Embrace the conversations with Carl Rogers, absorb the wisdom shared, and actively participate in the self-assessment activities. By doing so, you will unlock the full potential of this book and embark on a transformative path towards becoming an empathetic, growth-oriented, and impactful leader.

Get ready to embark on a 10-day journey that will challenge, inspire, and empower you. Let this book be your guide as you discover the transformative power of empathy and personal growth. Together, let's make a commitment to create meaningful change and cultivate a leadership style that fosters empathy, growth, and personal transformation.

Section 4: Chapter List

Chapter 1: The Art of Active Listening

1.1 Introduction

Active listening is not merely hearing words but fully engaging with the speaker's thoughts, emotions, and concerns. It is a powerful skill that builds trust, understanding, and fosters empathy in various interpersonal interactions, especially in the workplace.

The essence of active listening lies in its transformative power to foster genuine understanding, connection, and empathy in interpersonal interactions. Active listening goes beyond simply hearing words; it involves immersing oneself in the speaker's message, both verbal and non-verbal, and responding in a way that validates and respects their experiences.

At its core, active listening is about being fully present and engaged in the conversation. It requires setting aside distractions, maintaining eye contact, and using attentive body language to communicate genuine interest and receptiveness. By demonstrating these behaviors, active listeners create a safe and supportive space where individuals feel comfortable sharing their thoughts, emotions, and concerns.

Active listening is characterized by a non-judgmental and non-interruptive approach. It entails suspending one's own biases, assumptions, and agendas, and instead focusing on understanding the speaker's perspective without imposing personal interpretations. Through active listening, leaders cultivate empathy by genuinely seeking to grasp the speaker's point of view, emotions, and underlying needs.

By actively listening, leaders gain a deeper understanding of their employees' challenges, strengths, and aspirations. They develop a heightened awareness of the nuances and intricacies of the workplace dynamics, which enables them to make more informed decisions and provide meaningful support. Active listening also builds trust and rapport between leaders and employees, as individuals feel valued, respected, and heard.

The essence of active listening lies in its ability to create an environment conducive to open and honest communication. It paves the way for collaborative problem-solving, conflict resolution, and the generation of innovative ideas. By actively listening, leaders foster a sense of psychological safety, where individuals feel comfortable expressing their thoughts, sharing diverse perspectives, and challenging the status quo.

Moreover, active listening nurtures empathy, which is the key to building strong and resilient relationships. By genuinely understanding and empathizing with others' experiences, leaders can connect on a deeper level and forge meaningful connections. This empathy extends beyond the workplace, positively impacting both personal and professional relationships, and contributing to a culture of compassion and understanding.

In this chapter, we explore how active listening can be applied in the context of a conversation between an employee and a leader. Through a carefully crafted dialogue between Lisa, the employee, and Alex, the leader, we illustrate the power of active listening in fostering empathy and addressing concerns effectively.

By emphasizing the importance of active listening, Chapter 1 sets the stage for the subsequent chapters, laying the groundwork for empathetic and growth-oriented leadership. It highlights the transformative impact that active listening can have on building trust, understanding, and fostering empathetic connections within the workplace. As leaders embrace active listening, they pave the way for open communication, enhanced collaboration, and meaningful transformations within their teams and organizations.

1.2 Dialogue between Lisa (Employee) and Alex (Leader)

Lisa: Alex, thank you for taking the time to meet with me. I've been feeling overwhelmed with my workload lately, and it's starting to affect my productivity. I wanted to discuss it with you and see if we can find a solution together.

Alex: Of course, Lisa. I'm here to listen and support you. Please go ahead and share your concerns. I'm all ears.

Lisa: Well, it feels like there's just too much on my plate right now. I'm struggling to meet deadlines, and it's causing a lot of stress. I want to deliver quality work, but I'm finding it challenging with the current workload.

Alex: I appreciate you opening up about this, Lisa. It sounds like you're dealing with a heavy workload, and it's taking a toll on you. I want you to know that your well-being is important to me. Can you tell me more about the specific challenges you're facing?

Lisa: One of the main challenges is that I often have conflicting priorities. It's difficult to manage multiple projects simultaneously and ensure that each one receives the attention it deserves.

I'm afraid that I might not meet everyone's expectations or deliver the best results.

Alex: I understand how conflicting priorities can be overwhelming. It's important for me to know that you're doing your best, and I appreciate your dedication. Let's work together to find a solution. How do you think we can address these challenges and better manage our workload?

Lisa: One thing that could help is revisiting the project deadlines and reevaluating their urgency. Perhaps we can prioritize tasks and redistribute some of the workload. It would also be beneficial to have regular check-ins to discuss progress and identify any potential roadblocks.

Alex: Thank you for your suggestions, Lisa. I believe reevaluating deadlines and establishing clear priorities is a sensible approach. I also agree that regular check-ins would provide an opportunity for us to address any challenges promptly. Your input is valuable, and I want to assure you that we'll find a solution that works for both of us.

1.3 Potential Positive Outcomes of Active Listening

The conversation between Lisa and Alex, facilitated by active listening, can lead to several potential outcomes:

1. **Increased Trust and Rapport:** Active listening creates a safe and supportive environment where Lisa feels valued, heard, and understood. This fosters a sense of trust and rapport between Lisa and Alex, strengthening their working relationship.

2. **Deeper Understanding:** Through active listening, Alex gains a deeper understanding of Lisa's challenges, conflicting priorities, and emotional state. This understanding allows him to empathize with her experiences and offer more targeted support.

3. **Problem Identification and Resolution:** By actively listening, Alex can identify the specific issues that Lisa is facing, such as an overwhelming workload and the fear of not meeting expectations. This enables them to collaboratively explore potential solutions and develop strategies to address these challenges.

4. **Enhanced Communication:** Active listening promotes effective communication, as both Lisa and Alex feel comfortable expressing their thoughts and concerns. This leads to clearer and more meaningful exchanges, reducing miscommunication and fostering a shared understanding of expectations and goals.

5. **Empowered Employee:** Through active listening, Alex empowers Lisa to take ownership of her challenges and contribute to finding solutions. Feeling heard and supported, Lisa gains confidence

in her ability to navigate her workload and actively participates in problem-solving.

6. **Improved Employee Well-being:** The active listening approach demonstrates to Lisa that her well-being is a priority for Alex. By addressing her concerns and offering support, Alex contributes to reducing her stress levels, enhancing job satisfaction, and promoting a healthier work-life balance.

7. **Strengthened Team Dynamics:** The positive outcomes of the conversation between Lisa and Alex can extend beyond their individual relationship. Through active listening, Alex sets a precedent for open communication, empathy, and collaboration within the team, fostering an environment of trust and support.

Overall, the conversation facilitated by active listening can result in increased trust, improved communication, enhanced problem-solving, and a more empowered and engaged employee. These outcomes contribute to a positive work environment, where individuals feel valued, supported, and motivated to achieve their best.

1.4 Potential Pitfalls of Active Listening

While active listening generally promotes positive outcomes, there can be potential negative outcomes if it is not practiced effectively or if certain challenges arise in the conversation between Lisa and Alex. Some potential negative outcomes could include:

1. **Misunderstandings:** Despite active listening, there is a possibility of misunderstandings occurring. If there are gaps in communication or if either party misinterprets the other's intentions or messages, it can lead to miscommunication and a lack of resolution to the concerns at hand.

2. **Inadequate Problem-Solving:** If active listening does not translate into effective problem-solving, the conversation may not lead to practical solutions for Lisa's workload challenges. This could be due to a lack of collaborative effort, insufficient exploration of alternatives, or a failure to address the root causes of the issues.

3. **Emotional Disconnection:** Although active listening is meant to foster empathy and understanding, there is a chance that the conversation between Lisa and Alex does not evoke an emotional connection. If Alex's responses come across as mechanical or insincere, it may hinder the development of a genuine empathetic connection, leaving Lisa feeling unheard or undervalued.

4. **Unresolved Concerns:** Despite active listening, there is a possibility that the conversation does not

result in a satisfactory resolution of Lisa's concerns. If the challenges she faces are deeply rooted or require broader organizational changes, they may remain unresolved, potentially leading to frustration and dissatisfaction.

5. **Reinforcing Power Imbalance:** If Alex does not approach the conversation with a genuine intention to listen and address Lisa's concerns, it can reinforce power imbalances in their relationship. This may lead to feelings of disempowerment or undermine the trust that active listening aims to cultivate.

6. **Lack of Follow-up or Action:** Active listening is most effective when it leads to concrete actions or changes. If the conversation does not result in follow-up actions or if Alex fails to implement agreed-upon solutions, it can erode trust and diminish the perceived value of the active listening process.

It is important to acknowledge that these potential negative outcomes can arise in various scenarios and are not specific to the conversation between Lisa and Alex. The key is for leaders to be aware of these potential pitfalls and actively work to address them, ensuring that active listening is practiced effectively and leads to positive and productive outcomes.

1.5 Self-Assessment: Active Listening Skills

Instructions: Assess your active listening skills by reflecting on your behaviors, attitudes, and approaches during conversations with others.

Rate yourself on each statement below, using a scale of 1 to 5, where 1 represents "Strongly Disagree" and 5 represents "Strongly Agree."

Be honest and consider your typical behaviors rather than isolated incidents. Once completed, review your responses to identify areas for improvement and set goals to enhance your active listening skills.

Rating Scale

- Strongly Disagree: 1

- Disagree: 2

- Neutral: 3

- Agree: 4

- Strongly Agree: 5

S. No	Statement	Rating
1	I give my full attention to the speaker during conversations.	
2	I maintain eye contact and use attentive body language.	
3	I refrain from interrupting during conversations.	
4	I ask open-ended questions to encourage the speaker.	
5	I paraphrase or summarize the speaker's main points.	
6	I acknowledge and validate the speaker's feelings.	
7	I focus on the speaker's message rather than my response.	
8	I actively listen to understand, even if I disagree.	
9	I am patient and allow the speaker to express themselves fully.	
10	I am aware of my biases and suspend judgment.	

Total Score

Scoring

- Add up your scores for each statement.

- A score between 10-20 suggests a need for improvement in active listening skills.

- A score between 21-30 indicates moderate proficiency in active listening skills.

- A score between 31-40 suggests strong active listening skills.

1.6 REFLECTION AND ACTION

Reflection

After delving into Chapter 1 on the art of active listening, take a moment to reflect on your current listening habits and the insights gained from this chapter. Consider the following reflection points:

1. **Awareness of Listening Habits:** Reflect on your current listening habits and behaviors. Are you an active listener who genuinely engages with others, or do you find yourself frequently distracted or interrupting? Be honest with yourself and acknowledge any areas for improvement.

2. **Impact of Active Listening:** Consider the impact of active listening on your relationships, both personal and professional. Reflect on the times when you felt truly heard and understood, and how it enhanced the quality of your interactions. Recognize the value of active listening in building trust, fostering empathy, and creating meaningful connections.

3. **Barriers to Active Listening:** Identify any barriers or challenges you may face when it comes to active listening. This could include internal factors like distractions or preconceived notions, as well as external factors such as time constraints or a lack of focus. Awareness of these barriers can help you address them effectively.

4. **Empathy and Understanding:** Reflect on your ability to empathize with others and truly understand their perspectives. Consider instances where active listening allowed you to gain deeper insights into someone's emotions, experiences, or challenges. Recognize the power of empathy in fostering connection and personal growth.

Action

Based on your reflection, develop an action plan to enhance your active listening skills. Consider the following steps:

1. **Cultivate Mindful Presence:** Practice being fully present in conversations, giving your undivided attention to the speaker. Minimize distractions, put away electronic devices, and maintain eye contact to demonstrate your attentiveness.

2. **Practice Reflective Listening:** Train yourself to actively reflect and paraphrase what the speaker is saying. This demonstrates your understanding and allows the speaker to feel heard and validated. Avoid jumping to conclusions or interrupting prematurely.

3. **Ask Open-Ended Questions:** Engage in conversations by asking open-ended questions that invite deeper reflection and discussion. This shows your interest in understanding the speaker's perspective and encourages them to share more.

4. **Suspend Judgment:** Be mindful of your biases and judgments, consciously setting them aside to create a non-judgmental space for active listening. Recognize that everyone has a unique perspective, and your role is to understand and empathize, rather than evaluate or criticize.

5. **Seek Feedback:** Request feedback from trusted individuals in your life regarding your active listening skills. This feedback can provide valuable insights into areas where you excel and areas that may require further improvement.

6. **Reflect and Evaluate:** Regularly reflect on your active listening experiences and evaluate your progress. Celebrate the times when you practice active listening effectively and identify areas where you can continue to grow.

Remember, the journey of mastering active listening is ongoing. Embrace the actions outlined above and integrate them into your daily interactions. With time and practice, you will cultivate stronger active listening skills, deepen your connections, and create a more empathetic and supportive environment for yourself and those around you.

1.7 Conclusion – Active Listening

Chapter 1 has laid the groundwork for understanding the importance of active listening in fostering empathy and effective communication. The concept of active listening serves as a pillar for building trust, understanding diverse perspectives, and nurturing personal and professional growth.

In the subsequent chapters, we will delve further into the transformative power of empathy, exploring additional concepts and strategies that build upon the foundation of active listening. By continuing to cultivate your active listening skills, you will be better equipped to create an environment where individuals feel valued, heard, and empowered.

So, as you conclude Chapter 1, take this opportunity to reflect on your self-assessment, set goals for improvement, and embrace the journey of becoming an empathetic leader who listens actively and fosters meaningful connections. Let us move forward, inspired by the potential of active listening to unlock personal and professional growth, as we continue our exploration of empathy, growth, and personal transformation.

Top of Form

Chapter 2: Creating Psychological Safety

2.1 Introduction

This chapter explores the vital concept of creating psychological safety within teams and organizations. Psychological safety is a foundational element that enables individuals to take risks, express their ideas, and engage in open and honest dialogue without fear of judgment or reprisal.

In this chapter, we delve into the profound impact of psychological safety on team dynamics, innovation, and overall organizational success. We examine how leaders can cultivate an environment that fosters psychological safety, allowing individuals to feel comfortable, respected, and empowered to contribute their unique perspectives and talents.

Through engaging dialogues and practical examples, we explore the elements and behaviors that contribute to the creation of psychological safety. We delve into the power of active listening, empathy, inclusivity, and trust-building strategies. By understanding and implementing these practices, leaders can establish a culture that encourages collaboration, risk-taking, and learning from failures.

Psychological safety not only nurtures creativity and innovation but also enhances individual and team well-being. When individuals feel psychologically safe, they are more likely to share their ideas, ask for help, and support one another. This fosters a sense of belonging, increases engagement, and promotes a positive work environment.

Within this chapter, we provide actionable strategies and exercises to help leaders create psychological safety within their teams. By fostering an environment where individuals feel psychologically safe, leaders empower their team members to fully contribute their skills and perspectives, resulting in improved performance, increased productivity, and overall team success.

As you embark on this chapter, be prepared to reflect on your current leadership approach and consider the ways in which you can create a psychologically safe environment. Embrace the principles and practices outlined here, and witness the transformative power of psychological safety in fostering trust, collaboration, and personal growth within your team and organization.

Get ready to explore the remarkable potential of creating psychological safety as we embark on a journey that will not only transform your leadership style but also shape a culture of trust, resilience, and innovation.

2.2 Dialogue between Lisa (Employee) and Alex (Leader)

Lisa: Alex, I have an idea I'd like to share with you, but I'm not sure if it's worthwhile. I'm afraid it might not be well-received or that I'll be judged for speaking up.

Alex: Thank you for your honesty, Lisa. I appreciate your willingness to share your idea. Please know that our team values open and honest communication, and I want you to feel comfortable expressing your thoughts. Your perspectives are valuable to our collective success.

Lisa: That's reassuring to hear, Alex. Well, I've been thinking about a new approach to our client onboarding process. I believe we can streamline it to provide a more efficient and seamless experience for our clients. However, I'm uncertain if it's the right time to bring it up or if my idea holds merit.

Alex: I genuinely appreciate your initiative, Lisa. Creating psychological safety is important to me as a leader. Your idea certainly holds merit, and I encourage you to share it with the team. Let's schedule a meeting where you can present your proposal.

We will create an environment where everyone feels comfortable sharing their thoughts and actively participates in the discussion.

Lisa: Thank you, Alex. I feel more at ease now knowing that my idea will be given a fair chance. It means a lot to me to have the support and encouragement to speak up.

Alex: You're welcome, Lisa. Creating psychological safety is essential for fostering innovation and growth within our team. I value your contributions and want to create an environment where everyone feels respected and empowered to share their ideas. Remember, your perspective matters, and I believe in your ability to make a meaningful impact.

2.3 Potential Positive Outcomes of Creating Psychological Safety

The creation of psychological safety within a team or organization can lead to several positive outcomes, as demonstrated in the dialogue between Lisa and Alex. Some potential positive outcomes of fostering psychological safety include:

1. **Increased Innovation:** When individuals feel psychologically safe, they are more likely to share their ideas and perspectives without fear of judgment or negative consequences. This openness fosters

a culture of innovation, where diverse ideas are encouraged, leading to creative problem-solving and fresh approaches.

2. **Enhanced Collaboration:** Psychological safety promotes collaboration by creating an environment where team members feel comfortable working together, sharing knowledge, and seeking input from others. Collaboration flourishes when individuals trust that their contributions will be valued and respected.

3. **Improved Communication:** Creating psychological safety encourages open and honest communication. Team members feel more comfortable expressing their thoughts, concerns, and suggestions, leading to clearer and more effective communication throughout the team. This can reduce misunderstandings, promote transparency, and foster a shared understanding of goals and expectations.

4. **Increased Engagement and Empowerment:** Psychological safety empowers team members to actively participate and contribute their unique skills and perspectives. When individuals feel safe to share their thoughts and take risks, they become more engaged in their work, leading to increased motivation, productivity, and job satisfaction.

5. **Stronger Relationships and Trust:** Psychological safety builds trust within teams. When individuals feel safe to be vulnerable, express their opinions, and admit mistakes, it fosters a sense of trust and authenticity. This trust strengthens relationships, improves collaboration, and creates a supportive and cohesive team dynamic.

6. **Learning and Growth:** A psychologically safe environment encourages a growth mindset, where individuals are more willing to take risks, seek feedback, and learn from failures. When mistakes are seen as opportunities for growth rather than sources of blame, it promotes continuous learning, improvement, and personal development.

7. **Well-being and Psychological Health:** Psychological safety positively impacts the well-being and psychological health of individuals within the team. When team members feel valued, respected, and supported, it reduces stress, promotes a positive work-life balance, and contributes to a healthier and more fulfilling work environment.

These potential positive outcomes highlight the significance of creating psychological safety. By cultivating an environment where individuals feel safe to express themselves and take risks, leaders can unleash the full potential of their teams, driving innovation, collaboration, and personal growth.Bottom of Form

2.4 POTENTIAL PITFALLS OF CREATING PSYCHOLOGICAL SAFETY

While creating psychological safety within a team or organization is highly beneficial, it's important to be aware of potential pitfalls that may arise. These pitfalls can hinder the establishment of a psychologically safe environment and impact team dynamics. Some potential pitfalls of creating psychological safety include:

1. **Lack of Accountability:** In some cases, a focus on psychological safety may unintentionally lead to a lack of accountability. If team members feel excessively protected from consequences or performance expectations, it can hinder individual and team growth. It's important to strike a balance between psychological safety and maintaining accountability for individual and collective goals.

2. **Ineffective Conflict Resolution:** While psychological safety encourages open dialogue and the sharing of diverse perspectives, it's essential to establish effective conflict resolution strategies. Without proper guidance and facilitation, conflicts can escalate, negatively impacting team dynamics and eroding psychological safety. Leaders should foster an environment where conflicts are addressed constructively and resolved in a respectful manner.

3. **Limited Diversity of Thought:** Psychological safety is aimed at encouraging everyone's voice to be heard. However, if not managed carefully, it can unintentionally lead to groupthink or limited diversity of thought. It's crucial to actively promote inclusivity and ensure that diverse perspectives and opinions are genuinely sought and valued.

4. **Over-Reliance on Consensus:** Psychological safety may create an environment where individuals are hesitant to challenge or dissent from the majority opinion. While consensus-building is valuable, it's important to encourage constructive dissent and critical thinking. Leaders should foster an environment where diverse viewpoints are respectfully debated and considered, even if consensus is not always reached.

5. **Misinterpretation of Psychological Safety:** Misinterpretation or misuse of the concept of psychological safety can occur. It's essential to have shared understanding and clarity around the expectations and boundaries within a psychologically safe environment. This helps prevent situations where individuals may use psychological safety as an excuse for inappropriate or unprofessional behavior.

6. **Unequal Distribution of Psychological Safety:** There is a risk that psychological safety may not be experienced equally by all team members. Factors such as power dynamics, hierarchical structures, and individual differences can influence the extent to which individuals feel psychologically safe to speak up. Leaders should be vigilant to ensure equitable opportunities for all team members to contribute and feel psychologically safe.

7. **Lack of Continuous Effort:** Creating and maintaining psychological safety requires ongoing effort and attention. It is not a one-time action but an ongoing process. If leaders become complacent or fail to consistently reinforce psychological safety, it can deteriorate over time. Continuous support, open communication, and modeling of psychological safety behaviors are essential to sustain a psychologically safe environment.

Awareness of these potential pitfalls allows leaders to proactively address them and create strategies to mitigate their impact. By actively managing these challenges, leaders can foster a truly psychologically safe environment that encourages open communication, innovation, collaboration, and personal growth within their teams.

2.5 SELF-ASSESSMENT: CREATING PSYCHOLOGICAL SAFETY

Instructions

- Assess your effectiveness in creating a psychologically safe work environment by reflecting on your behaviors, attitudes, and practices.

- Rate yourself on each statement below, using a scale of 1 to 5, where 1 represents "Strongly Disagree" and 5 represents "Strongly Agree."

- Be honest and consider your typical behaviors and actions. Once completed, review your responses to identify areas for improvement and set goals to enhance psychological safety within your team.

Rating Scale

- Strongly Disagree: 1

- Disagree: 2

- Neutral: 3

- Agree: 4

- Strongly Agree: 5

S. No	Statement	Rating
1	I actively encourage open and honest communication within my team.	
2	I listen attentively to team members' ideas and perspectives.	
3	I provide constructive feedback and create growth opportunities.	
4	I am approachable and accessible to team members.	
5	I actively seek diverse viewpoints and value different perspectives.	
6	I encourage risk-taking and do not punish failure or mistakes.	
7	I promote a culture of collaboration and value every team member's contribution.	
8	I address conflicts in a constructive and respectful manner.	
9	I promote inclusivity and equal opportunity for all.	
10	I model vulnerability and authenticity in the workplace.	

Total Score

Scoring

Add up your scores for each statement.

- A score between 10-20 suggests a need for improvement in creating psychological safety.

- A score between 21-30 indicates moderate effectiveness in creating psychological safety.

- A score between 31-40 suggests strong effectiveness in creating psychological safety.

2.6 REFLECTION AND ACTION

Reflection

After exploring Chapter 2 on creating psychological safety, take a moment to reflect on your current practices and the insights gained from this chapter. Consider the following reflection points:

1. **Awareness of Psychological Safety:** Reflect on your awareness of psychological safety within your team or organization. Consider whether individuals feel comfortable expressing their opinions, taking risks, and making mistakes without fear of negative consequences. Acknowledge any areas where psychological safety may be lacking.

2. **Impact of Psychological Safety:** Consider the impact of psychological safety on team dynamics, innovation, and overall performance. Reflect on the times when you have experienced or observed psychological safety, and how it contributed to trust, collaboration, and the ability to share diverse perspectives. Recognize the value of creating an

environment where individuals feel safe to be authentic and take risks.

3. **Barriers to Psychological Safety:** Identify any barriers or challenges that may hinder the creation of psychological safety. This could include hierarchical structures, fear of judgment or retaliation, lack of open communication channels, or a culture that does not value diverse opinions. Recognize these barriers to address them effectively.

4. **Trust and Empowerment:** Reflect on your ability to build trust and empower others within your team or organization. Consider instances where you have fostered trust and created an environment where individuals feel empowered to speak up, share ideas, and contribute fully. Recognize the importance of trust and empowerment in establishing psychological safety.

Action

Based on your reflection, develop an action plan to enhance the creation of psychological safety. Consider the following steps:

1. **Foster Open Communication:** Encourage open and honest communication within your team or organization. Create channels for individuals to share their thoughts, concerns, and ideas freely.

Actively listen, validate perspectives, and provide opportunities for everyone to contribute.

2. **Lead by Example:** Demonstrate vulnerability and authenticity as a leader. Share your own mistakes and failures, and openly acknowledge them as learning opportunities. By modeling openness and acceptance, you create a safe space for others to do the same.

3. **Encourage Diverse Perspectives:** Actively seek out and value diverse perspectives within your team or organization. Create opportunities for individuals to express their unique viewpoints and encourage respectful dialogue. Embrace the richness that comes from diverse backgrounds, experiences, and ideas.

4. **Provide Feedback and Recognition:** Offer constructive feedback and recognition that focuses on growth and improvement. Create a culture where feedback is seen as a learning opportunity and recognition is given for effort, progress, and resilience. Encourage individuals to learn from mistakes and celebrate their successes.

5. **Establish Psychological Safety Norms:** Collaboratively establish norms and expectations that promote psychological safety within your team or organization. This could include agreements around respectful communication,

active listening, non-judgment, and confidentiality. Regularly revisit and reinforce these norms.

6. **Reflect and Adapt:** Regularly reflect on the psychological safety within your team or organization and evaluate your progress. Seek feedback from team members and adjust your actions as needed. Continuously strive to improve and adapt your practices to create an environment that fosters psychological safety.

Remember, creating psychological safety is an ongoing effort that requires commitment and continuous improvement. Embrace the actions outlined above and integrate them into your leadership approach. By nurturing psychological safety, you will empower individuals, foster collaboration, and create an environment where everyone feels valued, heard, and able to contribute their best work.

2.7 Conclusion – Creating Psychological Safety

In Chapter 2, we explored the profound impact of creating psychological safety within teams and organizations. We delved into the importance of fostering an environment where individuals feel safe, respected, and empowered to contribute their unique perspectives and ideas. Through this journey, we have uncovered the transformative power of psychological safety and its implications for team dynamics, innovation, and personal growth.

Creating psychological safety requires intentional effort and a commitment to fostering an inclusive and supportive work environment. It involves cultivating open communication, active listening, empathy, and trust-building practices. By creating psychological safety, leaders lay the foundation for collaboration, learning, and high-performance teams.

Throughout this chapter, we discussed the potential positive outcomes of creating psychological safety. These include increased innovation, enhanced collaboration, improved communication, increased engagement and empowerment, stronger relationships and trust, learning and growth, as well as improved well-being and psychological health.

However, it is important to recognize that creating psychological safety may also present challenges. As leaders, we need to be mindful of potential pitfalls, such as a lack of accountability, ineffective conflict resolution, limited diversity of thought, misinterpretation of psychological safety, unequal distribution of safety, and the need for continuous effort.

Moving forward, it is crucial to actively apply the principles and strategies discussed in this chapter. Leaders must commit to fostering psychological safety by encouraging open communication, embracing diverse perspectives, addressing conflicts constructively, and promoting inclusivity. By doing so, leaders cultivate an environment where team members feel safe to take risks, share ideas, and learn from failures.

As you conclude Chapter 2, reflect on your current practices in creating psychological safety. Identify areas where you excel and acknowledge your strengths. Furthermore, consider the potential pitfalls and challenges you may face. Set goals to enhance psychological safety within your team, and continuously refine your leadership approach to foster a psychologically safe work environment.

Remember, creating psychological safety is an ongoing journey. By embracing the principles and practices outlined in this chapter, you are taking a significant step toward becoming an empathetic and effective leader who nurtures a culture of trust, collaboration, and personal growth. Continue to prioritize psychological safety and witness the transformative impact it has on your team's success and well-being.

Chapter 3: Understanding Emotional Intelligence

3.1 Introduction

Welcome to Chapter 3 of "Coffee with Carl Rogers: Conversations on Empathy, Growth, and Personal Transformation." In this chapter, we delve into the fascinating realm of emotional intelligence and its profound influence on effective leadership and personal growth.

Emotional intelligence, often referred to as EQ, is the ability to recognize, understand, and manage our own emotions as well as the emotions of others. It encompasses a range of skills, including self-awareness, self-regulation, empathy, and relationship management. Developing emotional intelligence is crucial for leaders as it enables them to navigate complex interpersonal dynamics, build strong relationships, and make sound decisions.

In this chapter, we will explore the different components of emotional intelligence and how they contribute to effective leadership. Through engaging dialogues and practical examples, we will delve into the importance of self-awareness in understanding our own emotions, managing stress, and making conscious choices in our behavior and responses.

Furthermore, we will examine the role of empathy in emotional intelligence, exploring how it enhances our ability to understand and connect with others on a deeper level. We will uncover strategies for developing and practicing empathy in leadership, fostering inclusivity, and promoting collaboration.

Additionally, we will explore the significance of self-regulation and emotional control in maintaining composure, managing conflicts, and making rational decisions even in challenging situations. We will discuss techniques for enhancing self-regulation and building resilience in the face of adversity.

Understanding emotional intelligence is not only essential for effective leadership but also for personal growth and well-being. By cultivating our emotional intelligence, we can improve our self-awareness, manage our emotions more effectively, and enhance our relationships both personally and professionally.

As you embark on this chapter, be prepared to reflect on your own emotional intelligence and its impact on your leadership approach. Embrace the conversations with Carl Rogers and the practical exercises provided to develop and enhance your emotional intelligence skills. By doing so, you will unlock the power of emotional intelligence and harness its potential to become a more empathetic, self-aware, and impactful leader.

Get ready to explore the transformative realm of emotional intelligence as we embark on a journey of self-discovery, growth, and enhanced leadership capabilities.

3.2 DIALOGUE BETWEEN LISA (EMPLOYEE) AND ALEX (LEADER)

Lisa: Alex, I've been feeling a bit overwhelmed lately with the workload and tight deadlines. It's been challenging to manage my emotions and stay focused.

Alex: Thank you for sharing, Lisa. It takes self-awareness to recognize when we're feeling overwhelmed. Remember, emotional intelligence plays a crucial role in managing our emotions effectively. Have you considered using some strategies to help regulate your emotions and reduce stress?

Lisa: I haven't really thought about it. What strategies do you recommend?

Alex: One effective strategy is practicing mindfulness. Taking short breaks throughout the day to focus on your breathing and center yourself can help reduce stress levels and improve your overall well-being. Additionally, setting realistic goals and prioritizing tasks can provide a sense of control and alleviate some of the pressure.

Lisa: How can I improve my self-awareness?

Alex: Take a moment each day for self-reflection. By checking in with yourself and paying attention to your thoughts, feelings, and bodily sensations, you can gain insights into your emotional state. Journaling or mindfulness exercises can also help develop self-awareness.

Lisa: That sounds helpful.

Alex: It's understandable that a heavy workload can be overwhelming. Emotional intelligence can help us manage these situations effectively. Have you considered utilizing self-regulation techniques as well to better cope with the workload?

Lisa: How can self-regulation help?

Alex: Self-regulation involves managing our own emotions and behaviors in response to different situations. When faced with a heavy workload, it can be beneficial to prioritize tasks, set realistic goals, and establish healthy boundaries. By practicing self-regulation, we can maintain focus, reduce stress, and achieve a better work-life balance.

Lisa: That sounds helpful, Alex. So, I should focus on managing my time and setting boundaries to avoid feeling overwhelmed?

Alex: Exactly, Lisa. Self-regulation allows you to take control of your workload and establish healthy habits. It's essential to recognize your limits, delegate tasks when possible, and communicate your needs to ensure a manageable workload. By doing so, you can enhance your productivity and well-being.

Lisa: I'll make an effort to practice self-regulation and establish healthier work habits, Alex. It seems like emotional intelligence can truly make a difference in managing work-related challenges.

Alex: Absolutely, Lisa. Emotional intelligence empowers us to effectively manage our emotions and behaviors, leading to improved performance and overall well-being. Remember, it's a continuous practice, and I'm here to support you as you develop your emotional intelligence skills.

3.3 Components of Emotional Intelligence

The components of emotional intelligence, often referred to as EQ, include:

1. **Self-Awareness:** Self-awareness is the ability to recognize and understand one's own emotions, strengths, weaknesses, values, and motivations. It involves being in tune with one's emotional state and having a clear understanding of how emotions impact thoughts, behavior, and decision-making.

2. **Self-Regulation:** Self-regulation involves the ability to manage and control one's emotions, impulses, and behaviors in response to different situations. It includes techniques for managing stress, adapting to change, delaying gratification, and maintaining composure in challenging circumstances.

3. **Motivation:** Motivation refers to the drive and passion to pursue goals and achievements. It involves setting and working towards meaningful objectives, maintaining a positive attitude, and persevering in the face of obstacles. Motivated individuals have a strong sense of purpose and are often proactive in their endeavors.

4. **Empathy:** Empathy is the capacity to understand and share the feelings, perspectives, and experiences of others. It involves actively listening, recognizing and validating others' emotions, and demonstrating compassion. Empathy enables individuals to build strong relationships, communicate effectively, and respond empathetically to others' needs.

5. **Social Skills:** Social skills encompass a range of interpersonal abilities that facilitate effective communication, collaboration, and relationship building. It includes skills such as active listening, verbal and non-verbal communication, conflict resolution, teamwork, and networking. Individuals with strong social skills can navigate social situations, inspire and influence others, and build meaningful connections.

These **five components** of emotional intelligence are interconnected and work together to enable individuals to understand, manage, and navigate their own emotions and those of others. Developing and enhancing these components can lead to improved self-awareness, better interpersonal relationships, effective communication, and overall success in personal and professional domains.

3.4 Potential Pitfalls of Emotional Intelligence

While emotional intelligence (EQ) offers numerous benefits, there are potential pitfalls that individuals should be aware of. Some of the potential pitfalls of emotional intelligence include:

1. **Emotional Manipulation:** Individuals with high emotional intelligence may possess the ability to understand and influence others' emotions. In some

cases, this can be misused to manipulate or deceive others for personal gain, which goes against the principles of ethical behavior and empathy.

2. **Overly Emotional Decision-Making:** Emotional intelligence emphasizes the importance of recognizing and managing emotions. However, relying solely on emotions in decision-making without considering logical reasoning and objective analysis can lead to biased or impulsive choices that may not be in the best interest of individuals or organizations.

3. **Emotional Exhaustion:** Individuals with high emotional intelligence may find themselves consistently engaged in managing their own emotions and responding empathetically to others. This can be emotionally draining if they neglect self-care and fail to establish healthy boundaries, leading to emotional exhaustion and burnout.

4. **Overemphasis on Likability:** High emotional intelligence can sometimes lead individuals to prioritize being liked by others over making tough decisions or providing critical feedback. This desire for approval can compromise their ability to address conflicts or provide honest evaluations, impacting their effectiveness as leaders.

5. **Emotional Overload:** People with strong emotional intelligence may become highly attuned to others' emotions, absorbing and carrying the emotional burdens of others. This can result in emotional overload and make it challenging to maintain personal well-being and boundaries.

6. **Ignoring Cognitive Processes:** Emotional intelligence primarily focuses on understanding and managing emotions. However, it's important not to disregard the cognitive processes involved in decision-making, critical thinking, and problem-solving. An overemphasis on emotions alone may lead to overlooking important cognitive factors.

7. **Misinterpretation of Others' Emotions:** Despite efforts to empathize, individuals with high emotional intelligence may still misinterpret or misread others' emotions. This can lead to misunderstanding, miscommunication, and potential conflicts if assumptions are made based on inaccurate interpretations.

Awareness of these potential pitfalls can help individuals navigate emotional intelligence effectively. It is crucial to strike a balance between emotional awareness and other cognitive abilities, maintain ethical conduct, establish healthy boundaries, and prioritize self-care to avoid the potential downsides of emotional intelligence.

3.5 SELF-ASSESSMENT ON EMOTIONAL INTELLIGENCE

Instructions

- Assess your level of emotional intelligence by rating yourself on each statement below.

- Use a scale of 1 to 5, where 1 represents "Strongly Disagree" and 5 represents "Strongly Agree."

- Reflect on your typical behaviors and responses in various situations.

- Once completed, review your responses to identify areas for improvement and set goals to enhance your emotional intelligence.

Rating Scale

- Strongly Disagree: 1

- Disagree: 2

- Neutral: 3

- Agree: 4

- Strongly Agree: 5

S. No	Component	Statement	Rating
1	Self-Awareness	I am aware of my own emotions and how they influence my thoughts and actions.	
2		I can accurately identify my strengths, weaknesses, values, and motivations.	
3		I am conscious of the impact my emotions have on others around me.	
4	Self-Regulation	I am able to manage my emotions effectively, especially in challenging or stressful situations.	
5		I can adapt to changes and remain composed under pressure.	
6		I have a strong sense of self-control and can resist impulsive reactions.	
7	Motivation	I am driven by meaningful goals and have a clear sense of purpose in my personal and professional life.	
8		I remain positive and resilient in the face of setbacks or obstacles.	

S. No	Component	Statement	Rating
9		I am proactive and take initiative to pursue my goals with determination.	
10	Empathy	I actively listen to others and strive to understand their perspectives and emotions.	
11		I can accurately pick up on non-verbal cues and emotional signals from others.	
12		I demonstrate compassion and understanding towards others' experiences and feelings.	
13	Social Skills	I communicate effectively, both verbally and non-verbally, in various situations.	
14		I am skilled at building and maintaining positive relationships with others.	
15		I am adept at resolving conflicts and working collaboratively in a team setting.	

Total Score	

Scoring

- Add up your scores for each component.

- A score between 5-10 suggests a need for improvement in that component of emotional intelligence.

- A score between 11-15 indicates moderate effectiveness in that component.

- A score between 16-20 suggests strong effectiveness in that component.

- Please rate yourself on a scale of 1 to 5 for each statement, where 1 represents "Strongly Disagree" and 5 represents "Strongly Agree."

Top of Form

3.6 REFLECTION AND ACTION

Reflection

After exploring Chapter 3 on understanding emotional intelligence, take a moment to reflect on your current understanding and practices related to emotional intelligence. Consider the following reflection points:

1. **Self-awareness:** Reflect on your level of self-awareness regarding your own emotions, strengths, and limitations. Consider how well you understand

your emotions, triggers, and how they impact your thoughts, behaviors, and relationships.

2. **Empathy and Understanding:** Evaluate your ability to empathize with others and understand their emotions, perspectives, and experiences. Consider instances where you have demonstrated empathy and recognized the emotions of others.

3. **Emotional Regulation:** Reflect on your ability to manage and regulate your own emotions effectively. Consider how well you handle stress, control impulsive reactions, and respond to challenging situations with emotional intelligence.

4. **Interpersonal Relationships:** Consider the quality of your interpersonal relationships and how effectively you navigate conflicts, communicate, and build connections. Reflect on your ability to express emotions assertively and listen actively.

Action

Based on your reflection, develop an action plan to enhance your emotional intelligence. Consider the following steps:

1. **Develop Self-Awareness:** Cultivate self-awareness by engaging in introspection and reflection. Practice mindfulness techniques that help you observe and understand your own emotions, triggers, and

patterns of behavior. Journaling or seeking feedback from trusted individuals can also contribute to self-awareness.

2. **Cultivate Empathy:** Focus on developing empathy by actively seeking to understand others' perspectives and emotions. Practice active listening, engage in perspective-taking exercises, and demonstrate genuine interest and compassion for others.

3. **Enhance Emotional Regulation:** Strengthen your emotional regulation skills by developing strategies to manage stress and regulate your emotions effectively. This may include deep breathing exercises, mindfulness practices, or seeking support from a therapist or coach.

4. **Improve Communication and Relationships:** Enhance your communication skills by practicing active listening, non-verbal cues, and assertive expression of emotions. Foster open and honest communication, build trust, and strive for understanding in your relationships.

5. **Seek Continuous Learning:** Engage in learning opportunities to further develop your emotional intelligence. Read books or articles, attend workshops or seminars, and seek feedback from others to gain new insights and perspectives.

6. **Practice Self-Reflection:** Regularly reflect on your emotions, behaviors, and interactions. Consider the impact of your emotions on yourself and others. Identify areas for growth and improvement, and set goals to enhance your emotional intelligence.

7. **Embrace Feedback:** Be open to feedback from others regarding your emotional intelligence. Seek feedback from trusted individuals and genuinely consider their perspectives. Use feedback as a tool for self-improvement and growth.

Remember, developing emotional intelligence is a continuous journey. Embrace the actions outlined above and integrate them into your daily life and interactions. By cultivating emotional intelligence, you will enhance your self-awareness, improve your relationships, and navigate challenges with greater resilience and empathy.

3.7 CONCLUSION – UNDERSTANDING EMOTIONAL INTELLIGENCE

In Chapter 3, we delved into the fascinating realm of emotional intelligence and its profound impact on effective leadership and personal growth. We explored the five key components of emotional intelligence: self-awareness, self-regulation, motivation, empathy, and social skills. Through this exploration, we have gained insights into the importance of emotional intelligence in various aspects of our lives.

Emotional intelligence serves as a powerful tool for self-awareness, allowing us to recognize and understand our own emotions, strengths, weaknesses, values, and motivations. By developing self-regulation skills, we can effectively manage our emotions, adapt to changes, and maintain composure even in challenging situations. Motivation, a vital component of emotional intelligence, fuels our drive to pursue meaningful goals and maintain a positive attitude in the face of obstacles.

Empathy, another crucial aspect, enables us to connect with others on a deeper level by understanding and sharing their emotions and experiences. It empowers us to actively listen, validate feelings, and demonstrate compassion. Lastly, social skills play a pivotal role in building and maintaining positive relationships, effective communication, and collaboration.

By understanding and developing emotional intelligence, we can enhance our self-awareness, manage our emotions effectively, build strong relationships, and navigate social interactions with finesse. Emotional intelligence equips us with the tools to become empathetic and influential leaders, capable of inspiring and motivating others.

As we conclude Chapter 3, it is essential to recognize that emotional intelligence is not a fixed trait but a skill that can be cultivated and refined over time. Through self-reflection, practice, and a commitment to personal growth, we can enhance our emotional intelligence and make positive changes in our lives.

Take the knowledge and insights gained from this chapter and apply them to your everyday interactions and leadership roles. Challenge yourself to deepen your self-awareness, regulate your emotions, foster empathy, and refine your social skills. Set goals to continuously improve your emotional intelligence, seeking feedback and guidance from trusted individuals along the way.

By embracing the principles and practices of emotional intelligence, you will unlock your full leadership potential, forge meaningful connections with others, and navigate the complexities of personal and professional relationships with greater effectiveness and authenticity. Remember, the journey of emotional intelligence is ongoing, and each step forward brings us closer to becoming the best versions of ourselves.

CHAPTER 4: PRACTICING UNCONDITIONAL POSITIVE REGARD

4.1 INTRODUCTION

Welcome to Chapter 4 of "Coffee with Carl Rogers: Conversations on Empathy, Growth, and Personal Transformation." In this chapter, we explore the transformative practice of Unconditional Positive Regard (UPR) and its profound impact on our relationships, personal growth, and well-being.

Unconditional Positive Regard is a concept rooted in the humanistic approach to psychology, championed by Carl Rogers. It involves cultivating an attitude of acceptance, empathy, and non-judgment towards ourselves and others, irrespective of their behaviors or circumstances. By practicing UPR, we create a safe and supportive space where individuals can truly be seen, heard, and accepted for who they are.

At its core, UPR involves embracing individuals with an unwavering positive regard, regardless of their actions, behaviors, or circumstances. It recognizes that every person has inherent worth and the capacity for growth and self-actualization. UPR goes beyond superficial acceptance and extends genuine empathy, understanding, and support to facilitate an environment where individuals can freely express themselves, explore their true selves, and work towards self-improvement.

The principles of Unconditional Positive Regard (UPR) guide the practice of UPR and create a foundation for building supportive, accepting relationships. The key principles of UPR include:

1. **Acceptance:** UPR emphasizes accepting individuals as they are, without judgment, conditions, or expectations. It involves embracing their unique qualities, experiences, and perspectives without trying to change or fix them.

2. **Non-Judgment:** UPR encourages suspending personal biases, preconceived notions, and evaluations of others. It involves refraining from labeling, categorizing, or criticizing individuals based on their behaviors or choices.

3. **Empathy:** UPR requires cultivating empathy, the ability to understand and share the feelings and experiences of others. It involves actively listening, seeking to understand, and validating others' emotions without trying to fix or dismiss them.

4. **Genuineness:** Practicing UPR involves being authentic and genuine in our interactions. It requires sincere engagement, honesty, and transparency. Genuine expressions of care, respect, and support contribute to an atmosphere of trust and authenticity.

5. **Unconditional Regard:** UPR extends positive regard to individuals regardless of their actions, behaviors, or circumstances. It recognizes the inherent worth and potential for growth in every person, emphasizing their value as human beings.

6. **Emotional Safety:** UPR fosters emotional safety by creating a non-threatening environment where individuals feel comfortable expressing themselves without fear of judgment, rejection, or negative consequences.

7. **Self-Acceptance:** UPR extends to oneself, emphasizing the importance of self-acceptance and self-compassion. It involves treating oneself with kindness, embracing strengths and weaknesses, and nurturing a positive self-image.

8. **Growth and Self-Actualization:** UPR supports individuals' personal growth and self-actualization by providing an accepting and supportive environment. It encourages individuals to explore their full potential, make choices aligned with their values, and pursue meaningful goals.

By embracing these principles, individuals can cultivate UPR in their relationships, creating spaces that promote acceptance, empathy, and growth. UPR supports the development of authentic connections, enhances psychological well-being, and contributes to a more compassionate and inclusive society.

4.2 DIALOGUE BETWEEN LISA (EMPLOYEE) AND ALEX (LEADER)

Lisa: Alex, I've been feeling really down lately. I made a mistake at work, and I can't stop beating myself up about it. I feel like I'm letting everyone down.

Alex: Lisa, I'm here for you. Remember, mistakes happen to everyone, and they don't define who you are. Let's talk about it. What happened?

Lisa: I missed an important deadline on a project, and it caused delays for the entire team. I feel like I've disappointed everyone, especially myself.

Alex: I understand that you're feeling disappointed, but it's important to recognize that mistakes are a part of the learning process. We all make them. What matters now is how we handle the situation and learn from it. You have the potential to grow from this experience.

Lisa: I appreciate your support, Alex, but I can't help but feel like I've let everyone down. I'm afraid of what they might think of me.

Alex: Lisa, it's crucial to remember that we all make mistakes, and it doesn't diminish your value or worth. I believe in your abilities and the contributions you bring to our team. Let's focus on finding a solution to the issue at hand and how we can prevent similar situations in the future.

Lisa: Thank you, Alex. Your understanding and support mean a lot to me. I'm just struggling with forgiving myself and moving forward.

Alex: It's completely normal to feel that way, Lisa. Remember, Unconditional Positive Regard means accepting yourself as you are, flaws and all. It's about treating yourself with kindness, compassion, and forgiveness. Let's work together to find strategies that can help you bounce back from this setback and grow stronger.

Lisa: I'll try my best to practice self-acceptance and learn from this experience. Your guidance and belief in me give me the confidence to move forward.

Alex: That's the spirit, Lisa. I have no doubt that you will overcome this challenge and emerge even stronger. Remember, I'm here to support you every step of the way.

In this dialogue, Alex demonstrates Unconditional Positive Regard towards Lisa. He acknowledges her mistake without judgment, offers empathy and understanding, and helps her shift her perspective from self-criticism to self-acceptance and growth. Through their conversation, they aim to create a safe and supportive space where Lisa can learn from her mistakes, embrace her worth, and work towards a solution with renewed confidence.

4.3 Potential Positive Outcomes of Practicing UPR

Practicing Unconditional Positive Regard (UPR) can lead to a range of positive outcomes in personal relationships, professional settings, and individual well-being. Some of the potential positive outcomes of practicing UPR include:

1. **Enhanced Empathy and Understanding:** UPR fosters empathy, allowing individuals to better understand and connect with others' experiences and emotions. This leads to improved communication, deeper connections, and more meaningful relationships.

2. **Increased Trust and Psychological Safety:** UPR creates an environment of acceptance and non-judgment, which builds trust and promotes psychological safety. When individuals feel safe to express themselves authentically without fear of criticism or rejection, they are more likely to be open and honest in their interactions.

3. **Improved Communication and Conflict Resolution:** Practicing UPR enhances communication skills, as individuals actively listen, validate emotions, and demonstrate understanding. This promotes effective conflict resolution, as conflicts are approached with empathy and a willingness to find mutually beneficial solutions.

4. **Nurturing Personal Growth and Self-Actualization:** UPR supports personal growth and self-actualization by creating a space where individuals can explore their true selves, embrace their strengths and weaknesses, and pursue their goals without fear of judgment. This encourages self-discovery, self-acceptance, and the realization of one's full potential.

5. **Greater Resilience and Emotional Well-being:** UPR contributes to increased resilience and emotional well-being. When individuals experience acceptance and understanding, they develop a stronger sense of self-worth and are better equipped to navigate challenges, cope with stress, and bounce back from setbacks.

6. **Positive Organizational Culture:** In professional settings, practicing UPR fosters a positive organizational culture. It encourages collaboration, respect, and appreciation among team members, leading to improved teamwork, employee engagement, and job satisfaction.

7. **Empowerment and Motivation:** UPR empowers individuals by recognizing their intrinsic worth and potential. This promotes self-belief, motivation, and a sense of agency to pursue personal and professional goals.

8. **Increased Compassion and Social Connection:** UPR cultivates compassion and nurtures a sense of interconnectedness. By practicing acceptance and empathy, individuals contribute to a more compassionate and inclusive society, fostering social connections and a sense of belonging.

It is important to note that the positive outcomes of practicing UPR may vary depending on individual circumstances and the context in which it is applied. However, overall, embracing UPR has the potential to create transformative effects, nurturing healthier relationships, personal growth, and a more compassionate and empathetic society.

4.4 POTENTIAL PITFALLS OF UPR

While Unconditional Positive Regard (UPR) has many benefits, there are potential pitfalls that individuals should be mindful of when practicing it. These pitfalls include:

1. **Enabling Negative Behavior:** In some cases, practicing UPR without setting appropriate boundaries

or providing constructive feedback can inadvertently enable negative or harmful behavior. It is important to balance acceptance and empathy with accountability and the encouragement of personal growth.

2. **Disregarding Personal Boundaries:** While UPR emphasizes acceptance, it is crucial to respect personal boundaries and avoid intruding on others' privacy or personal space. Respecting individual autonomy and their need for privacy is essential for maintaining healthy relationships.

3. **Emotional Exhaustion:** Constantly providing unconditional support and empathy to others can be emotionally demanding. Individuals who consistently prioritize others' well-being without attending to their own self-care may experience emotional exhaustion or burnout. It is important to maintain a balance between supporting others and taking care of oneself.

4. **Inauthenticity:** Practicing UPR should come from a place of genuine empathy and understanding. However, if individuals force themselves to be accepting or suppress their own emotions or needs, it can lead to inauthentic interactions and emotional incongruence. It is crucial to strike a balance between empathy and authenticity.

5. **Ignoring Red Flags:** Excessive focus on UPR can sometimes cause individuals to overlook red flags or warning signs in relationships or situations. While acceptance is important, it is also essential to recognize and respond to behaviors that may be harmful or detrimental.

6. **Misinterpretation as Approval:** UPR should not be confused with unconditional approval. While individuals can practice acceptance and empathy, it is essential to communicate boundaries and expectations clearly to avoid misinterpretation that may lead to enabling or harmful consequences.

7. **Neglecting Personal Growth:** While UPR supports the growth of others, individuals should also prioritize their own personal growth and self-improvement. Practicing UPR should not be at the expense of neglecting personal goals, boundaries, or well-being.

8. **Cultural and Contextual Considerations:** UPR may need to be practiced with cultural sensitivity and consideration for individual contexts. Different cultures, social norms, or situations may have unique expectations or boundaries that should be respected and understood.

It is important to approach the practice of UPR mindfully, considering the specific circumstances and the well-being of all individuals involved. Striking a balance between acceptance, empathy, and personal growth is key to harnessing the positive potential of UPR while avoiding potential pitfalls.

4.5 Self-Assessment on UPR

Instructions

- Review the tabular format of the UPR self-assessment, which consists of various aspects related to practicing UPR, corresponding statements, and a rating column.

- For each aspect and statement, read the statement carefully and reflect on your own behavior and attitudes towards practicing UPR. Consider how frequently you engage in the described behaviors or demonstrate the mentioned qualities.

- Assign a rating to each statement based on your self-perception and assessment of your current practice of UPR. Use the rating scale provided, where 1 represents "Strongly Disagree" and 5 represents "Strongly Agree."

- Rate each statement honestly and without judgment. Try to assess your practice of UPR as objectively as possible, considering real-life situations and interactions.

Rating Scale

- Strongly Disagree: 1

- Disagree: 2

- Neutral: 3

- Agree: 4

- Strongly Agree: 5

S. No	Aspect	Statement	Rating
1	Acceptance	I approach others with acceptance, embracing their unique qualities and perspectives.	
		I refrain from passing judgment or criticism towards others.	
2	Empathy	I actively listen to others and seek to understand their feelings and experiences.	
		I validate others' emotions and demonstrate understanding.	
3	Personal Boundaries	I respect others' personal boundaries and privacy.	
		I communicate my own boundaries clearly and assertively.	

S. No	Aspect	Statement	Rating
4	Balancing Support and Feedback	I provide support and empathy while also offering constructive feedback when necessary.	
		I encourage personal growth and accountability in others.	
5	Authenticity	I am genuine and authentic in my interactions, expressing my true thoughts and emotions.	
		I remain true to myself while practicing UPR.	
6	Self-Care	I prioritize self-care and ensure I am not neglecting my own well-being while supporting others.	
		I recognize my own needs and seek support when necessary.	
7	Cultural Sensitivity	I consider cultural differences and adapt my approach to practicing UPR accordingly.	
		I respect and honor the cultural norms and boundaries of others.	

Total Average Score	

Scoring

1. **Excellent Practice:** A total average rating of 4 or above indicates a consistently high level of practicing UPR. It reflects a strong ability to demonstrate acceptance, empathy, respect for personal boundaries, and authenticity in interactions.

2. **Good Practice:** A total average rating between 3 and 3.9 suggests a solid practice of UPR, with room for growth and refinement. It signifies a moderate ability to embrace acceptance, empathy, and other UPR principles.

3. **Development Needed:** A total average rating below 3 suggests a need for improvement in practicing UPR. It indicates a lower level of ability in demonstrating acceptance, empathy, respecting personal boundaries, or authenticity.

Remember, the success criteria are meant to provide a general assessment of your current practice of UPR. The focus should be on personal growth and continuous improvement, rather than achieving a specific numerical rating. Use self-assessment as a starting point to identify areas for development and set goals to enhance your practice of UPR.

4.6 REFLECTION AND ACTION

Reflection

After completing the Unconditional Positive Regard (UPR) self-assessment, take a moment to reflect on your ratings and the overall assessment of your practice of UPR. Consider the following questions:

1. **Strengths:** What aspects of practicing UPR do you feel confident in? Which statements did you rate highly?

2. **Growth Areas:** What aspects of practicing UPR do you believe need improvement? Which statements did you rate lower?

3. **Patterns:** Are there any patterns or common themes in your ratings? Do you notice any consistent strengths or challenges in your practice of UPR?

4. **Impact:** How do you think your current practice of UPR affects your relationships, communication, and overall well-being?

Action

Based on your reflection, develop an action plan to enhance your practice of UPR. Consider the following steps:

1. **Identify Areas for Improvement:** Focus on the aspects or statements where you rated lower or believe improvement is needed. These are the areas that present opportunities for growth.

2. **Set Specific Goals:** Establish specific goals related to the identified areas for improvement. For example, if you rated low on empathy, a goal could be to actively practice active listening and seeking to understand others' perspectives.

3. **Strategies and Practices:** Determine strategies and practices that can help you enhance your practice of UPR. This could include reading books on empathy, attending workshops or training sessions, or seeking guidance from a mentor or therapist.

4. **Implementation and Integration:** Put your action plan into practice by incorporating UPR principles into your daily interactions. Practice empathy, non-judgment, and acceptance in your conversations with others. Monitor your progress and make adjustments as needed.

5. **Self-Reflection:** Regularly reflect on your progress and reassess your practice of UPR. Consider the impact of your efforts on yourself and those around you. Continue to learn, grow, and adapt as you refine your practice of UPR.

Remember that personal growth is a journey, and it takes time and effort to enhance your practice of UPR. Be patient and compassionate with yourself as you work towards becoming a more accepting and empathetic individual. By consciously practicing UPR, you can create a positive impact on your relationships, communication, and overall well-being.

4.7 Conclusion – Unconditional Positive Regard (UPR)

In Chapter 4, we explored the concept of Unconditional Positive Regard (UPR) and its significance in fostering healthy relationships and personal growth. Throughout this chapter, we learned that UPR involves accepting oneself and others without judgment, cultivating empathy, respecting personal boundaries, and promoting authenticity.

By practicing UPR, we create an environment that encourages open communication, trust, and understanding. We recognize the inherent worth and potential for growth in every individual, embracing their uniqueness and offering support without conditions. UPR enables us to form deeper connections, resolve conflicts empathetically, and promote personal development.

The journey of practicing UPR begins with self-reflection and self-acceptance. By embracing our own imperfections and practicing self-compassion, we become better equipped to extend acceptance and empathy to others. As we actively listen, seek to understand, and validate emotions, we create safe spaces for authentic expression and emotional well-being.

However, we must also remain mindful of potential pitfalls associated with UPR. Enabling negative behavior, disregarding personal boundaries, and neglecting our own well-being are challenges we need to navigate. Striking a balance between acceptance and accountability is crucial in maintaining healthy relationships and promoting personal growth.

As leaders, practicing UPR becomes even more important. By fostering a culture of acceptance, empathy, and non-judgment in our teams and organizations, we create environments where individuals feel valued, supported, and empowered to reach their full potential. UPR contributes to enhanced communication, collaboration, and overall well-being in the workplace.

In conclusion, UPR is a transformative practice that promotes acceptance, empathy, and personal growth. By cultivating a mindset of unconditional acceptance and applying UPR principles in our interactions, we create a positive impact not only on ourselves but also on the lives of those around us. Let us continue to embrace UPR, recognizing the power it holds to create profound change in our relationships and our world.

CHAPTER 5: NURTURING A GROWTH MINDSET

5.1 INTRODUCTION

In Chapter 5, we delve into the concept of a growth mindset and its profound impact on personal and professional development. A growth mindset is the belief that abilities and intelligence can be developed through effort, dedication, and a willingness to learn from failures and setbacks. It is a mindset that embraces challenges, persists in the face of obstacles, and seeks opportunities for growth.

In this chapter, we explore the transformative power of adopting a growth mindset and how it can lead to increased resilience, motivation, and achievement. We will examine the characteristics of a growth mindset and learn practical strategies to nurture this mindset within ourselves and those we lead.

By cultivating a growth mindset, we shift our perspective from viewing challenges as insurmountable obstacles to seeing them as opportunities for growth and learning. We embrace a belief in our own potential and recognize that intelligence and abilities can be developed through deliberate practice and perseverance.

Throughout this chapter, we will explore the ways in which a growth mindset can positively impact our personal and professional lives. We will discover how it influences our approach to problem-solving, decision-making, and goal-setting. Additionally, we will explore the role of feedback, effort, and the power of yet in fostering a growth mindset.

By the end of this chapter, you will gain a deeper understanding of the concept of a growth mindset and its significance in fostering personal and professional growth. You will be equipped with practical strategies to cultivate and nurture a growth mindset in yourself and others. So, let's embark on this journey of transformation and embrace the power of a growth mindset to unlock our full potential.

5.2 Dialogue between Lisa (Employee) and Alex (Leader)

Lisa: Alex, I've been facing a lot of challenges at work lately, and it's been really discouraging. I feel like no matter how hard I try, I can't seem to make any progress.

Alex: I understand how frustrating that can be, Lisa. It's important to remember that challenges are a part of growth and development. Instead of viewing them as roadblocks, what if we saw them as opportunities for learning and improvement?

Lisa: I guess that's a different way to think about it. But sometimes, it's hard to stay positive when things don't go as planned. I start doubting my abilities and wondering if I'm just not cut out for this.

Alex: I can understand why you might feel that way, but let me share something with you. Have you heard of the concept of a growth mindset? It's the belief that our abilities and intelligence can be developed through effort and learning. Instead of thinking that we have fixed capabilities, we recognize that we can always improve and grow.

Lisa: That sounds interesting, Alex. How can I cultivate a growth mindset?

Alex: One way is to embrace challenges as opportunities for growth. When you encounter a difficult task or setback, instead of feeling defeated, see it as a chance to learn and develop new skills. Focus on the process rather than just the outcome.

Lisa: So, it's about being open to learning from failures and setbacks?

Alex: Exactly. Embrace the idea that mistakes are part of the learning process. Instead of dwelling on them, reflect on what you can learn from them and how you can improve. Remember, failure is not a reflection of your worth or intelligence but an opportunity to grow stronger.

Lisa: That's a refreshing perspective, Alex. What about effort and persistence?

Alex: Effort and persistence are key components of a growth mindset. Recognize that progress takes time and dedication. Instead of getting discouraged by temporary setbacks, maintain a positive attitude and keep pushing forward. See effort as a pathway to improvement and celebrate the progress you make along the way.

Lisa: I can see how adopting a growth mindset can change my outlook. It's about embracing challenges, learning from failures, and putting in the effort to grow. Thank you, Alex, for introducing me to this concept.

Alex: You're welcome, Lisa. Remember, developing a growth mindset is a journey, and it takes practice. But with time and perseverance, you'll find yourself approaching challenges with renewed confidence and a belief in your ability to grow. I'll be here to support you every step of the way.

In this dialogue, Alex introduces Lisa to the concept of a growth mindset and encourages her to shift her perspective on challenges and setbacks. They discuss the importance of embracing challenges, learning from failures, and putting in the effort to grow. Through this conversation, Lisa begins to see the value of cultivating a growth mindset and the positive impact it can have on her personal and professional development.

5.3 Potential Positive Outcomes of Nurturing a Growth Mindset

Nurturing a growth mindset can lead to a range of positive outcomes, both personally and professionally. Here are some potential positive outcomes of embracing and cultivating a growth mindset:

1. **Increased Resilience:** A growth mindset fosters resilience by teaching individuals to see setbacks and failures as opportunities for learning and growth. It helps individuals bounce back from challenges, setbacks, and obstacles with renewed determination and a positive attitude.

2. **Continuous Learning and Development:** Embracing a growth mindset encourages a love for learning and a desire for self-improvement. Individuals with a growth mindset actively seek out new knowledge, skills, and experiences, which leads to personal and professional development.

3. **Improved Problem-Solving Skills:** A growth mindset fosters a proactive approach to problem-solving. It encourages individuals to view problems as solvable and to seek creative solutions. With a growth mindset, individuals are more likely to think critically, explore different perspectives, and find innovative ways to overcome challenges.

4. **Increased Motivation and Drive:** Individuals with a growth mindset are often more motivated and driven to achieve their goals. They believe in their ability to improve and are willing to put in the effort and perseverance required to reach their full potential. A growth mindset fuels intrinsic motivation and a sense of purpose.

5. **Enhanced Self-Confidence:** Embracing a growth mindset nurtures a sense of self-confidence. When individuals believe in their capacity to learn and grow, they develop a positive self-image and greater self-assurance. This increased self-confidence empowers individuals to take on new challenges and step out of their comfort zones.

6. **Stronger Relationships and Collaboration:** A growth mindset promotes collaboration and positive relationships. Individuals with a growth mindset value the growth and development of others, creating an

environment of support and encouragement. They are more likely to embrace feedback, collaborate effectively, and foster a sense of teamwork.

7. **Adaptability and Agility:** Nurturing a growth mindset equips individuals with the adaptability and agility needed to navigate change and uncertainty. They are more open to new ideas, willing to explore different approaches, and comfortable with taking calculated risks. This mindset enables individuals to embrace change as an opportunity for growth and innovation.

8. **Increased Achievement and Success:** Ultimately, nurturing a growth mindset can lead to increased achievement and success. Individuals who believe in their capacity to learn, grow, and overcome obstacles are more likely to persevere, set ambitious goals, and achieve significant outcomes in their personal and professional lives.

By cultivating a growth mindset, individuals can unlock their full potential, overcome challenges, and continuously improve themselves. The positive outcomes of embracing a growth mindset extend beyond personal development and can positively impact relationships, teamwork, and overall success.

5.4 POTENTIAL PITFALL OF NURTURING A GROWTH MINDSET

While nurturing a growth mindset is generally beneficial, there are potential pitfalls that individuals should be aware of. These pitfalls include:

1. **Overemphasis on Success:** While a growth mindset encourages learning from failures, there can be a danger of becoming too focused on achieving success. This can lead to setting unrealistic expectations, constant self-criticism, and a fear of failure, which may hinder growth and enjoyment of the learning process.

2. **Disregarding Effort and Process:** A growth mindset emphasizes the importance of effort and perseverance. However, there is a risk of overlooking the significance of effective strategies, proper planning, and the process of learning. Overemphasizing effort alone without considering effective approaches may lead to inefficiency or stagnation.

3. **Ignoring Realistic Assessment:** While a growth mindset encourages belief in one's ability to improve, it's essential to balance this with a realistic assessment of skills and limitations. Ignoring areas where improvement may be challenging or not aligning with personal strengths and values can lead to frustration and unrealistic expectations.

4. **Comparison and Competition:** In the pursuit of growth, individuals may fall into the trap of comparing themselves to others or engaging in excessive competition. This can shift the focus from personal growth to external validation, creating feelings of inadequacy or fostering an unhealthy sense of rivalry.

5. **Neglecting Self-Care:** Nurturing a growth mindset requires dedication and effort, but it's crucial to prioritize self-care and well-being. Overextending oneself, neglecting rest and relaxation, or ignoring personal boundaries can lead to burnout and hinder the overall growth process.

6. **Fixed Mindset Triggers:** Despite efforts to cultivate a growth mindset, individuals may still encounter triggers or situations that evoke a fixed mindset. These triggers can include setbacks, criticism, or comparison to others. Awareness of these triggers is important to actively counteract them and maintain a growth-oriented mindset.

7. **Lack of External Support:** Nurturing a growth mindset is greatly facilitated by a supportive environment. If individuals do not receive adequate encouragement, feedback, or resources from their surroundings, it can impede their growth and make it challenging to maintain a strong growth mindset.

Awareness of these potential pitfalls can help individuals navigate the journey of nurturing a growth mindset more effectively. It's important to find a balance between ambition and realistic expectations, prioritize self-care, seek a supportive environment, and remain mindful of the learning process rather than solely focusing on outcomes.

5.5 SELF-ASSESSMENT ON NURTURING A GROWTH MINDSET

Instructions: For each statement, rate your agreement based on your current mindset and behaviors. Use the following rating scale:

1 – Strongly Disagree | 2 – Disagree| 3 – Neutral| 4 – Agree | 5 – Strongly Agree

S. No	Statement	Rating
1	I believe that intelligence and abilities can be developed through effort and learning.	
2	I embrace challenges as opportunities for growth and learning.	
3	I persist in the face of obstacles and setbacks.	
4	I view failures as learning experiences and opportunities for improvement.	
5	I seek out feedback and constructive criticism to help me grow.	

S. No	Statement	Rating
6	I am open to trying new strategies and approaches to achieve better outcomes.	
7	I celebrate the success and progress of others without feeling threatened or jealous.	
8	I am aware of my strengths and weaknesses and actively work on improving areas of growth.	
9	I believe that dedication and effort are more important than innate talent or intelligence.	
10	I am motivated to continuously learn and develop new skills.	
11	I maintain a positive attitude even when facing challenges or setbacks.	
12	I practice self-reflection to identify areas for improvement and set goals for personal growth.	
13	I support and encourage others in their pursuit of growth and development.	
14	I embrace change and see it as an opportunity for personal growth.	
15	I am willing to take risks and step out of my comfort zone to learn and grow.	
16	I prioritize self-care and well-being while pursuing personal and professional growth.	

Total Average Score	

Scoring

1. Calculate the total score by summing up the ratings for all the statements.

2. Divide the total score by the number of statements to obtain the average rating.

3. Reflect on your average rating and consider the following interpretation:

   - Excellent Practice: An average rating of 4 or above indicates a strong commitment to nurturing a growth mindset and actively applying its principles.

   - Good Practice: An average rating between 3 and 3.9 suggests a solid practice of nurturing a growth mindset, with room for further growth and development.

   - Development Needed: An average rating below 3 indicates a need for improvement in nurturing a growth mindset. Consider focusing on specific areas where growth is needed.

Use the self-assessment as a tool for self-reflection and identify areas where you can further enhance your practice of nurturing a growth mindset. Set goals and strategies to foster continuous growth and development in your personal and professional life. Remember, the purpose of the self-assessment is to guide self-improvement, so be kind and patient with yourself as you embark on this journey of nurturing a growth mindset.

5.6 REFLECTION AND ACTION

Reflection

After completing the self-assessment on nurturing a growth mindset, take a moment to reflect on your ratings and the overall assessment of your mindset and behaviors. Consider the following reflection points:

1. **Strengths:** Identify areas where you scored highly and demonstrated a strong commitment to nurturing a growth mindset. Acknowledge the qualities and behaviors that reflect your belief in growth, resilience, and continuous learning.

2. **Growth Areas:** Identify areas where you scored lower or feel there is room for improvement in nurturing a growth mindset. Reflect on the reasons behind these ratings and consider the specific mindset shifts or behaviors that you can focus on to foster growth.

3. **Patterns:** Look for patterns or trends in your ratings. Do you notice consistent strengths or areas that require more attention? Understanding these patterns can provide valuable insights into your current mindset and areas for development.

4. **Impact:** Reflect on how your current mindset and behaviors impact your personal and professional life. Consider the effects on your motivation, resilience, relationships, and overall growth. Recognize the importance of nurturing a growth mindset and the potential benefits it can bring.

Action

Based on your reflection, develop an action plan to further nurture and develop a growth mindset. Consider the following steps:

1. **Set Specific Goals:** Identify specific goals related to nurturing a growth mindset based on your reflection. Focus on areas where you want to strengthen your beliefs, behaviors, or responses to challenges.

2. **Mindset Shift:** Identify specific mindset shifts that you want to cultivate. For example, embrace failures as learning opportunities, see challenges as growth experiences, and believe in the power of effort and perseverance.

3. **Behavior Change:** Determine specific behaviors you can adopt to foster a growth mindset. This may include seeking feedback, embracing curiosity, practicing self-reflection, setting learning goals, and celebrating progress.

4. **Learning and Development:** Seek out resources, workshops, or courses that can support your growth mindset journey. Engage in activities that expand your knowledge, enhance your skills, and expose you to new perspectives.

5. **Accountability and Support:** Share your goals and aspirations with a trusted friend, mentor, or colleague. Establish accountability measures to keep you on track and seek their support and guidance throughout the process.

6. **Practice and Reflection:** Consistently practice the mindset shifts and behaviors you have identified. Regularly reflect on your progress, celebrate achievements, and learn from setbacks or challenges along the way.

Remember, nurturing a growth mindset is a continuous journey of self-discovery and development. Be patient and compassionate with yourself as you work towards fostering a growth-oriented mindset. Embrace challenges, seek learning opportunities, and believe in your capacity to learn and grow. By taking intentional actions and maintaining a growth mindset, you can unlock your full potential and achieve personal and professional growth.

5.7 CONCLUSION – NURTURING A GROWTH MINDSET

In Chapter 5, we explored the concept of nurturing a growth mindset and its transformative potential. We learned that a growth mindset is a belief in the ability to develop and improve through effort, resilience, and a dedication to continuous learning. Throughout this chapter, we examined the positive outcomes of embracing a growth mindset and the potential pitfalls to be mindful of along the journey.

By nurturing a growth mindset, we unlock our potential for personal and professional growth. Embracing challenges as opportunities for learning, persisting in the face of setbacks, and seeking feedback and constructive criticism become foundational principles of our mindset. We cultivate a love for learning, set ambitious goals, and believe in our capacity to achieve them through dedicated effort and perseverance.

The practice of a growth mindset empowers us to approach life with resilience, adaptability, and a sense of possibility. We become more open to new experiences, perspectives, and strategies, allowing us to embrace change and seek opportunities for growth. Our motivation becomes intrinsic, driven by a desire for self-improvement and a belief in our ability to continuously evolve.

Nurturing a growth mindset not only benefits us individually but also has a profound impact on our relationships, teams, and organizations. It fosters a culture of learning, collaboration, and innovation, where individuals are encouraged to take risks, support each other's growth, and embrace the collective potential for development.

As we conclude this chapter, let us carry forward the insights gained and actively cultivate a growth mindset in our lives. Embrace challenges, view failures as stepping stones to success, and persist in the pursuit of personal and professional growth. By nurturing a growth mindset, we unlock our limitless potential and create a pathway for continuous learning, resilience, and achievement. Let us embrace the journey ahead, ready to embrace growth and seize the opportunities that come our way.

Top of Form

Chapter 6: The Power of Vulnerability

6.1 Introduction

In Chapter 6, we delve into the transformative power of vulnerability. Vulnerability is the courageous act of opening ourselves up to emotional risk, embracing our imperfections, and expressing our true thoughts and feelings. It is through vulnerability that we create deeper connections, foster empathy, and unlock our true potential.

In this chapter, we explore the profound impact vulnerability can have on our personal and professional lives. We examine the barriers and fears that often prevent us from embracing vulnerability and discuss strategies to cultivate and harness its power. By understanding and embracing vulnerability, we can foster an environment of trust, authenticity, and growth.

Throughout this chapter, we will explore the importance of vulnerability in leadership and its role in building strong relationships and effective communication.

We will debunk myths and misconceptions surrounding vulnerability, and delve into the ways it can enhance our resilience, empathy, and capacity for personal development.

By embracing vulnerability, we create space for authenticity, genuine connections, and meaningful collaboration. We learn to let go of the need for perfection and embrace our true selves. Vulnerability allows us to learn from failures, seek support, and embrace the discomfort that comes with growth. It is through vulnerability that we find strength and resilience to navigate challenges and seize opportunities.

Throughout this chapter, we will delve into practical strategies to cultivate vulnerability in our lives. We will explore ways to create safe environments where vulnerability is celebrated and encouraged. By embracing vulnerability within ourselves and fostering it in our teams and organizations, we can create a culture that values openness, trust, and continuous growth.

So, let us embark on this journey of embracing vulnerability. By embracing our vulnerabilities and allowing ourselves to be seen, we unlock the potential for deeper connections, personal growth, and meaningful contributions. Let us explore the power of vulnerability and discover how it can transform our lives and the lives of those around us.

6.2 DIALOGUE BETWEEN LISA (EMPLOYEE) AND ALEX (LEADER)

Lisa: Alex, I've been wanting to talk to you about something that's been weighing on my mind. It's a bit uncomfortable for me, but I trust that you'll listen and understand.

Alex: Thank you for coming to me, Lisa. I appreciate your trust. Please know that you can always share your thoughts and concerns with me. What's on your mind?

Lisa: Well, recently I've been struggling with a project I'm working on. I feel overwhelmed and uncertain about the direction I'm taking. I worry that I might not meet the expectations, and it's causing me a lot of stress.

Alex: Thank you for opening up, Lisa. I can understand how challenging it can be to navigate through uncertainty and self-doubt. I want you to know that it's okay to feel this way, and you're not alone. In fact, I've experienced similar feelings in the past.

Lisa: Really? I didn't expect that. It's reassuring to know that even as a leader, you've faced similar challenges. It makes me feel less alone and more understood.

Alex: Absolutely, Lisa. As a leader, it's important for me to create an environment where everyone feels comfortable being vulnerable and sharing their struggles. We all face challenges, and it's through embracing vulnerability that we can build deeper connections and support each other.

Lisa: I appreciate that, Alex. It's refreshing to have a leader who encourages vulnerability. It makes me feel safe to express my concerns without fear of judgment or repercussions.

Alex: That's exactly what I aim for, Lisa. By accepting vulnerability and creating a safe space, we foster an environment where we can grow together. It's through these moments of openness that we can offer support, guidance, and learn from one another.

Lisa: I agree, Alex. It's encouraging to know that I can seek guidance from you and that we can work together to overcome challenges. This conversation has helped alleviate some of my stress, and I feel more confident in tackling the project now.

Alex: I'm glad to hear that, Lisa. Remember, vulnerability is a strength, and by embracing it, we create opportunities for growth and collaboration. If there's anything else you'd like to discuss or if you need further support, please don't hesitate to reach out.

Lisa: Thank you, Alex. I truly appreciate your openness and support. This conversation has definitely strengthened our connection, and I feel more comfortable approaching you with any future concerns or ideas.

Alex: You're most welcome, Lisa. Building these connections and fostering a culture of acceptance and vulnerability is essential to our success as a team. Together, we can navigate challenges and create a positive and supportive work environment.

In this dialogue, Lisa demonstrates vulnerability by expressing her struggles and concerns about a project to Alex. Alex, as a leader, responds with empathy and understanding, sharing his own experiences and reassuring Lisa that she is not alone. By accepting and validating Lisa's vulnerability, they create a deeper connection and a safe space for open communication. This dialogue highlights the power of accepting vulnerability in leadership and how it can foster trust, understanding, and stronger connections within a team.

6.3 POTENTIAL POSITIVE OUTCOMES OF ACCEPTING VULNERABILITY

Accepting vulnerability can lead to several positive outcomes in both personal and professional contexts. Some potential positive outcomes include:

1. **Increased Trust and Connection:** When individuals show vulnerability and open up about their fears, challenges, and emotions, it creates an atmosphere of trust and authenticity. Others can relate to and empathize with their vulnerability, fostering deeper connections and stronger relationships.

2. **Enhanced Communication and Collaboration:** Embracing vulnerability encourages open and honest communication. It allows individuals to express their thoughts, concerns, and ideas more freely, leading to improved collaboration, better problem-solving, and the exploration of innovative solutions.

3. **Improved Problem-Solving and Creativity:** Vulnerability often leads to a willingness to take risks and explore new ideas. By accepting vulnerability, individuals become more open to diverse perspectives and alternative approaches, fostering creativity and innovation in problem-solving.

4. **Increased Learning and Growth:** Vulnerability creates opportunities for personal and professional growth. By admitting limitations and seeking help or feedback, individuals can acquire new knowledge and skills. It allows for a growth mindset, as individuals are open to learning from mistakes and failures.

5. **Strengthened Emotional Intelligence:** Accepting vulnerability requires emotional self-awareness and regulation. It promotes the development of emotional intelligence by understanding and managing one's own emotions and empathizing with the emotions of others. This leads to improved interpersonal relationships and effective leadership.

6. **Resilience and Adaptability:** Embracing vulnerability builds resilience as individuals learn to navigate uncertainty, setbacks, and change. It fosters an ability to bounce back from challenges and adapt to new circumstances, increasing overall resilience and agility.

7. **Supportive Work Environment:** When vulnerability is accepted and encouraged, it creates a supportive work environment where individuals feel safe to be their authentic selves. This can lead to higher job satisfaction, increased employee engagement, and improved overall well-being.

8. **Positive Influence and Leadership:** Leaders who accept vulnerability set a powerful example for their team members. By modeling vulnerability, leaders create an environment that encourages others to embrace their own vulnerabilities, fostering a culture of openness, trust, and growth.

By accepting vulnerability, individuals can experience these positive outcomes, leading to stronger relationships, personal growth, and improved team dynamics. It enables a supportive and thriving environment where individuals can bring their whole selves, leading to enhanced creativity, collaboration, and success.

6.4 POTENTIAL PITFALLS OF ACCEPTING VULNERABILITY

While accepting vulnerability can lead to positive outcomes, it's important to be aware of potential pitfalls that individuals may encounter. Some potential pitfalls of accepting vulnerability include:

1. **Fear of Judgment and Rejection:** When individuals show vulnerability, there is always a risk of facing judgment or rejection from others. This fear may deter individuals from being open and authentic, leading to self-censorship and the avoidance of sharing their true thoughts and feelings.

2. **Emotional Overexposure:** Accepting vulnerability requires individuals to expose their emotions and inner thoughts. There is a risk of becoming emotionally overwhelmed or feeling exposed, particularly if vulnerability is not reciprocated or respected by others.

3. **Exploitation or Manipulation:** In some situations, individuals who show vulnerability may be taken

advantage of or manipulated by others. This can occur when trust is broken or when vulnerability is used against them for personal gain or control.

4. **Perceived Weakness or Lack of Competence:** There is a societal misconception that vulnerability equates to weakness or incompetence. Some individuals may worry that embracing vulnerability will be perceived as a lack of strength or competence, potentially impacting their professional reputation or opportunities.

5. **Limited Support or Understanding:** Not everyone may respond positively or understand the significance of vulnerability. Some individuals may dismiss or downplay the importance of vulnerability, leading to a lack of support or a dismissive response when individuals open up.

6. **Vulnerability Hangover:** After sharing vulnerable thoughts or experiences, individuals may experience a "vulnerability hangover" characterized by feelings of regret, anxiety, or self-doubt. This can occur when individuals question whether they should have shared certain information or worry about how others perceive them.

7. **Lack of Boundaries:** Accepting vulnerability requires setting healthy boundaries to protect one's emotional well-being. Without clear boundaries,

individuals may find themselves overwhelmed by others' emotions or struggles, leading to emotional exhaustion or blurred personal and professional boundaries.

It is important to approach vulnerability with care and discernment. While embracing vulnerability can be empowering, individuals should be mindful of their emotional well-being and assess the trustworthiness of the people they choose to be vulnerable with. Building a supportive network and seeking professional guidance, if needed, can help navigate the potential pitfalls and ensure that vulnerability is expressed in a healthy and beneficial manner.

6.5 SELF-ASSESSMENT: ACCEPTING AND EMBRACING VULNERABILITY

Instructions

Please read each statement below and rate yourself on a scale of 1 to 5 based on how well you believe you accept and embrace vulnerability in various areas of your life. Be honest with your responses. After rating each statement, calculate your total score and refer to the scoring guide to interpret your results.

Rating Scale

1 – Strongly Disagree | 2 – Disagree| 3 – Neutral|
4 – Agree | 5 – Strongly Agree

S.No	Statement	Rating (1-5)
1	I am comfortable expressing my emotions openly.	
2	I am willing to admit my mistakes and learn from them.	
3	I actively seek feedback from others to improve myself.	
4	I share my fears and insecurities with trusted individuals.	
5	I am open to asking for help when I need it.	
6	I am comfortable with being seen as imperfect.	
7	I embrace uncertainty and take risks even when it feels uncomfortable.	
8	I create a safe and non-judgmental environment for others to express their vulnerabilities.	
9	I am open to sharing my personal experiences to connect with others.	
10	I am willing to engage in difficult conversations with authenticity and vulnerability.	

S.No	Statement	Rating (1-5)
11	I accept and learn from constructive criticism without becoming defensive.	
12	I take responsibility for my actions and apologize when necessary.	
13	I am open to trying new things, even if there is a chance of failure.	
14	I trust others enough to share my deepest thoughts and feelings.	
15	I embrace vulnerability as a strength rather than a weakness.	

Total Score: _______________ (Add up all your ratings)

Interpretation

- If your total score falls between **1 and 15**, it indicates a low acceptance and embracing of vulnerability. There may be opportunities for growth in this area.

- If your total score falls between **16 and 30**, it suggests a moderate acceptance and embracing of vulnerability. There may be some areas where you can further develop your ability to embrace vulnerability.

- If your total score falls between **31 and 45**, it indicates a high acceptance and embracing of vulnerability. You are comfortable with vulnerability and have developed a strong capacity for openness and authenticity.

Use this self-assessment as a starting point to reflect on your current relationship with vulnerability. Identify areas where you may need to further embrace vulnerability and explore strategies to cultivate a deeper acceptance of vulnerability in your life. Remember that vulnerability is a continuous journey, and by actively working on it, you can create deeper connections, personal growth, and a more fulfilling life.

6.6 REFLECTION AND ACTION

Reflection

After completing the Accepting and Embracing Vulnerability self-assessment, take a moment to reflect on your scores and what they reveal about your relationship with vulnerability. Consider the following reflection points:

1. **Awareness of Vulnerability:** Reflect on your level of awareness and acceptance of vulnerability in your life. Consider how comfortable you are with being open, authentic, and expressing your true thoughts and emotions. Acknowledge any areas where you may struggle with embracing vulnerability.

2. **Impact of Vulnerability:** Evaluate the impact of your acceptance or resistance to vulnerability on your

personal and professional relationships. Consider how it affects your ability to connect with others, communicate effectively, and build trust. Recognize any patterns or areas where embracing vulnerability could have a positive impact.

3. **Barriers to Vulnerability:** Identify any barriers or fears that may hinder your acceptance and embracing of vulnerability. These barriers could be related to past experiences, societal expectations, or personal beliefs. Recognize these barriers to address and overcome them effectively.

4. **Recognizing Growth Opportunities:** Reflect on areas where you scored lower and opportunities for growth in accepting and embracing vulnerability. Consider how embracing vulnerability could enhance your personal development, relationships, and overall well-being. Identify specific areas where you would like to focus your efforts.

Action

Based on your reflection, develop an action plan to strengthen your acceptance and embracing of vulnerability. Consider the following steps:

1. **Self-Reflection and Journaling:** Engage in self-reflection and journaling to explore your thoughts, emotions, and experiences related to vulnerability.

Use this practice as a tool for deeper self-awareness and understanding of your relationship with vulnerability.

2. **Practicing Vulnerability:** Challenge yourself to practice vulnerability in small, manageable ways. This could involve sharing your feelings or opinions with trusted individuals, expressing your authentic self, or engaging in honest conversations with empathy and openness.

3. **Seeking Support:** Reach out to supportive individuals who can provide guidance and encouragement as you navigate vulnerability. Share your experiences and fears, and seek their advice or insights. Having a strong support system can make the journey of embracing vulnerability more manageable.

4. **Learning and Education:** Invest time in learning about vulnerability, its benefits, and strategies to cultivate it. Read books, attend workshops or seminars, or listen to podcasts that focus on vulnerability and personal growth. Expand your knowledge to gain new perspectives and insights.

5. **Mindfulness and Emotional Regulation:** Develop mindfulness practices to cultivate emotional awareness and regulation. This will enable you to navigate uncomfortable emotions that may arise

from embracing vulnerability and respond to them in a healthy and constructive manner.

6. **Celebrating Progress:** Recognize and celebrate your progress in embracing vulnerability. Acknowledge moments where you have shown vulnerability and reflect on the positive outcomes that resulted. Celebrating small wins will motivate you to continue on this journey of growth.

Remember, embracing vulnerability is a continuous process that requires patience and self-compassion. Be kind to yourself as you navigate the challenges and celebrate the successes along the way. By actively working on accepting and embracing vulnerability, you can create deeper connections, personal growth, and a more fulfilling life.

6.7 Conclusion – The Power of Vulnerability

In this chapter, we explored the transformative power of vulnerability and its profound impact on our personal and professional lives. We recognized that vulnerability is not a sign of weakness but a strength that allows us to embrace our authentic selves, connect with others on a deeper level, and foster personal growth.

Throughout our journey, we learned that accepting and embracing vulnerability is not always easy. It requires courage to step outside our comfort zones, share our fears and insecurities, and allow ourselves to be seen as imperfect. However, the rewards that come from embracing vulnerability are truly remarkable.

By accepting vulnerability, we create a safe space for open and honest communication, where trust and authenticity thrive. We build deeper connections with others as they witness our genuine selves, and we encourage them to do the same. Through vulnerability, we strengthen our relationships, cultivate empathy, and foster a sense of belonging.

Embracing vulnerability also enables us to learn and grow. By acknowledging our mistakes, seeking feedback, and being open to new experiences, we expand our horizons and develop resilience. Vulnerability pushes us to step into the unknown, take risks, and pursue personal development with an open heart and mind.

However, we must also be mindful of the potential pitfalls that vulnerability can bring. Fear of judgment, emotional overexposure, and exploitation are among the challenges we may encounter. It is essential to set boundaries, seek support from trusted individuals, and be discerning in sharing our vulnerabilities.

As we conclude this chapter, let us remember that vulnerability is a continuous journey. It is not about achieving perfection or always being vulnerable but rather about cultivating a healthy balance and embracing vulnerability when it serves us and our relationships. Each step we take towards vulnerability is an opportunity for growth, connection, and self-discovery.

By embracing vulnerability, we unlock our true potential and invite others to do the same. Let us create a world where vulnerability is celebrated, where authenticity is valued, and where we can all thrive as our authentic selves. As we continue on our journey, let us carry the lessons of this chapter with us, embracing vulnerability as a powerful force for personal and collective transformation.

Chapter 7: Conflict Resolution Through Empathy

7.1 Introduction

Welcome to Chapter 7, where we delve into the transformative power of empathy in conflict resolution. Conflict is an inevitable part of human interaction, whether in our personal relationships or professional environments. However, by approaching conflicts with empathy, we can foster understanding, build bridges, and find resolutions that honor the needs and perspectives of all parties involved.

In this chapter, we will explore how empathy can be a guiding principle in navigating conflicts effectively. We will delve into the importance of active listening, perspective-taking, and emotional intelligence in fostering empathetic responses during conflicts. By honing these skills, we can create a safe and supportive environment for dialogue, leading to deeper understanding and sustainable resolutions.

Conflict resolution through empathy goes beyond mere compromise; it seeks to uncover the underlying emotions, concerns, and values that drive the conflict. Through empathy, we develop the ability to truly listen to others, acknowledging their experiences and emotions without judgment. This creates a foundation of trust and openness, essential for finding common ground and moving towards mutually beneficial solutions.

Throughout this chapter, we will explore practical strategies and techniques for applying empathy in conflict resolution. We will examine case studies and engage in interactive exercises to deepen our understanding and refine our empathetic responses. By expanding our empathy toolkit, we empower ourselves to transform conflicts into opportunities for growth, connection, and collaboration.

Embracing conflict resolution through empathy also aligns with Carl Rogers's teachings, as it emphasizes the importance of creating a safe and empathetic space for self-expression and understanding. By incorporating empathy into our conflict resolution practices, we honor the principles of acceptance, authenticity, and empathy that underpin Rogers's humanistic approach.

As we embark on this chapter, let us recognize that conflict resolution is not about eliminating disagreements but about transforming them into opportunities for growth and connection. Through empathy, we can foster harmonious relationships, build bridges across differences, and pave the way for sustainable solutions.

May this chapter provide you with valuable insights, practical tools, and a deeper understanding of conflict resolution through empathy. Together, let us explore the transformative potential of empathy in resolving conflicts and creating a more compassionate and understanding world.

7.2 Dialogue between Lisa (Employee) and Alex (Leader)

Lisa: Alex, I wanted to talk to you about a conflict that has been arising between me and one of my colleagues. I feel like our communication has been breaking down, and it's causing tension and frustration. I'm not sure how to resolve it.

Alex: I'm glad you brought this up, Lisa. Conflict is a natural part of working in a team, and it's important that we address it proactively. Can you tell me more about the situation and what you've been experiencing?

Lisa: Well, it seems like we have different approaches to completing tasks, and we often clash when making decisions. Instead of listening to each other's perspectives, we tend to get defensive and shut down any ideas that don't align with our own. It's creating a negative atmosphere, and it's affecting our productivity.

Alex: I understand how challenging that can be. It seems like there is a breakdown in communication and a lack of empathy. To address this, I think it's crucial for us to practice active listening and perspective-taking. Let's try an exercise to help us better understand each other's viewpoints.

Lisa: That sounds like a good approach, Alex. How should we start?

Alex: Let's take turns sharing our thoughts and concerns without interruption. I'll go first, and then I'd like you to summarize what you think I said before sharing your own perspective. This way, we can ensure that we're truly listening and understanding each other.

Lisa: That sounds fair. Please go ahead, Alex.

Alex: Thank you, Lisa. I feel that our differing approaches stem from our unique experiences and expertise. While it's natural to have different opinions, I realize that I haven't fully considered your insights in the past. I want to change that and create a more inclusive environment where we value diverse perspectives.

Lisa: Thank you for sharing, Alex. If I understand correctly, you acknowledge that our differences can be valuable and that you're open to considering my perspective. I appreciate that. From my side, I believe our different approaches can complement each other if we find a way to integrate them. I'm committed to actively listening to your ideas and finding common ground for collaboration.

Alex: Thank you, Lisa. Your summary accurately reflects my thoughts. I'm glad to hear your commitment to active listening and collaboration. I believe that by embracing empathy and understanding each other's viewpoints, we can find innovative solutions and create a more harmonious work environment.

Lisa: I agree, Alex. Let's make a conscious effort to practice empathy and communicate openly moving forward. I believe this will not only help resolve our current conflicts but also strengthen our working relationship overall.

Alex: Absolutely, Lisa. By fostering a culture of empathy, we can create an environment where conflicts become opportunities for growth and collaboration. Together, we can find solutions that benefit both ourselves and the team.

In this dialogue, Lisa and Alex demonstrate the importance of active listening, empathy, and perspective-taking in addressing conflicts. They recognize the need to understand each other's viewpoints and commit to practicing empathy to foster a more inclusive and collaborative work environment. By embracing these principles, they set the stage for effective conflict resolution and improved working relationships.

7.3 POTENTIAL POSITIVE OUTCOMES OF CONFLICT RESOLUTION THROUGH EMPATHY

1. **Enhanced Understanding:** Conflict resolution through empathy can lead to a deeper understanding of each other's perspectives, experiences, and underlying needs. This understanding promotes empathy and compassion, allowing individuals to see beyond their own viewpoints and develop a more comprehensive picture of the situation.

2. **Improved Communication:** Empathy helps create an open and non-judgmental environment for communication. By actively listening and acknowledging each other's emotions and concerns, individuals can engage in more constructive and effective dialogue. This improved communication fosters trust and allows for more productive problem-solving.

3. **Strengthened Relationships:** Conflict resolution through empathy builds stronger relationships

based on mutual respect and understanding. By demonstrating empathy, individuals validate each other's feelings and experiences, leading to increased trust and a sense of connection. This, in turn, cultivates a more positive and supportive working or personal relationship.

4. **Collaborative Solutions:** When empathy is applied during conflict resolution, individuals are more likely to seek collaborative solutions rather than resorting to win-lose scenarios. By considering multiple perspectives and finding common ground, creative and mutually beneficial solutions can be achieved. Empathy promotes a mindset of collaboration and teamwork, enhancing problem-solving outcomes.

5. **Increased Emotional Intelligence:** Conflict resolution through empathy contributes to the development of emotional intelligence. Individuals become more attuned to their own emotions and those of others, leading to improved self-awareness and empathy skills. This heightened emotional intelligence allows for better regulation of emotions during conflicts and more empathetic responses towards others' emotions.

6. **Reduced Tension and Stress:** Empathy in conflict resolution helps diffuse tension and reduce stress levels. When individuals feel heard, understood,

and validated, they experience a sense of relief and a decrease in emotional distress. This can create a more positive and harmonious environment, benefiting everyone involved.

7. **Personal Growth and Learning:** Conflict resolution through empathy offers opportunities for personal growth and learning. By engaging in empathetic listening and understanding, individuals gain new insights, broaden their perspectives, and develop greater self-awareness. They can identify areas for personal improvement and cultivate skills that contribute to their overall emotional intelligence and interpersonal effectiveness.

Overall, conflict resolution through empathy brings about positive outcomes such as enhanced understanding, improved communication, strengthened relationships, collaborative solutions, increased emotional intelligence, reduced tension, and personal growth. By embracing empathy in conflict resolution, individuals can transform conflicts into opportunities for growth, connection, and positive change.

7.4 POTENTIAL PITFALLS OF CONFLICT RESOLUTION THROUGH EMPATHY

While conflict resolution through empathy is a valuable approach, it is important to acknowledge the potential pitfalls that may arise in the process. These pitfalls include:

1. **Emotional Overload:** In some cases, individuals involved in the conflict may become overwhelmed by the emotions elicited during the empathetic exchange. Strong emotions can hinder effective communication and problem-solving, making it challenging to reach a resolution.

2. **Imbalance of Power:** Empathy requires a balance of power and a willingness to understand each other's perspectives. However, in situations where there is a significant power imbalance, such as hierarchical structures or unequal dynamics, one party may struggle to express their needs or concerns freely, limiting the effectiveness of empathy in resolving the conflict.

3. **Lack of Boundaries:** Empathy should be practiced with clear boundaries to ensure that individuals' emotional well-being is protected. Without boundaries, there is a risk of emotional exhaustion, as individuals may take on excessive emotional burdens or sacrifice their own needs in the pursuit of resolving the conflict.

4. **Misinterpretation of Intentions:** Despite the best intentions, there is a possibility of misinterpreting the intentions behind empathetic

actions. Misunderstandings can arise, leading to further misunderstandings or conflicts. It is crucial to communicate openly and clarify intentions to prevent such misinterpretations.

5. **Ineffective Implementation:** Applying empathy without the necessary skills and strategies may result in ineffective conflict resolution. While empathy is important, it should be complemented by active listening, effective communication, and problem-solving techniques to facilitate a successful resolution.

6. **Dependency on Empathy Alone:** Relying solely on empathy without considering other conflict resolution strategies can limit the potential for a comprehensive and balanced solution. Empathy should be integrated with other techniques, such as negotiation, compromise, and problem-solving, to address the underlying issues and reach a mutually beneficial resolution.

7. **Unrealistic Expectations:** Expecting immediate resolution or a complete elimination of conflicts through empathy alone can lead to disappointment and frustration. Conflict resolution is a process that requires time, effort, and ongoing commitment from all parties involved.

It is important to be aware of these potential pitfalls and actively work to address them while practicing conflict resolution through empathy. By doing so, individuals can navigate conflicts more effectively and create an environment conducive to understanding, growth, and collaboration.

7.5 Self-Assessment – Are You Ready to Handle Conflicts Through Empathy

Instructions

Read each statement below and rate yourself on a scale of 1 to 5, indicating the extent to which you agree with each statement. Be honest and reflect on your typical behavior and attitudes in conflict situations.

On the scale of 1 to 5, the ratings can be interpreted as follows:

1 – Strongly Disagree | 2 – Disagree | 3 – Neutral | 4 – Agree | 5 – Strongly Agree

S.No	Statement	Rating (1-5)
1	I am open to listening to others' perspectives and emotions during conflicts.	
2	I can effectively manage my own emotions and remain calm during conflicts.	
3	I actively seek to understand the underlying needs and concerns of others in conflicts.	

S.No	Statement	Rating (1-5)
4	I can separate my personal biases and judgments from conflicts and empathize with others' experiences.	
5	I am skilled at active listening, paraphrasing, and reflecting back others' emotions during conflicts.	
6	I believe that conflicts can be opportunities for growth and understanding.	
7	I am willing to acknowledge my own role in conflicts and take responsibility for my actions.	
8	I can identify and address power imbalances in conflicts, ensuring that all parties have a voice.	
9	I am able to establish clear boundaries and protect my own emotional well-being during conflicts.	
10	I actively seek to find collaborative solutions that meet the needs of all parties involved in conflicts.	

Scoring

- Add up your ratings for all the statements.

- The higher the total score, the more ready you are to handle conflicts through empathy.

- The maximum possible score is 50.

Scoring Interpretation

40-50: Excellent

30-39: Good

20-29: Average

10-19: Below Average

1-9: Needs Improvement

7.6 Reflection and Action

As we come to the end of Chapter 7, take a moment to reflect on the content covered and your personal journey in understanding and applying conflict resolution through empathy. Consider the following questions:

1. **What insights have you gained about the role of empathy in conflict resolution?**

Reflect on the key concepts and strategies discussed in this chapter. How have these insights deepened your understanding of the importance of empathy in resolving conflicts? What specific examples or experiences come to mind that highlight the transformative power of empathy?

2. **How have you personally applied empathy in conflict resolution situations?**

Recall instances where you have consciously applied empathy to resolve conflicts in your own life. Consider the outcomes of those situations and the impact of your empathetic approach. How did empathy contribute to better understanding, collaboration, and resolution?

3. What challenges or obstacles have you encountered in applying empathy during conflicts?

Reflect on any difficulties or barriers you have faced when attempting to use empathy in conflict resolution. Are there specific situations or factors that hindered your empathetic responses? What have you learned from these challenges and how can you overcome them in the future?

Action

Based on your reflection, consider the following actions to further develop your ability to handle conflicts through empathy:

1. **Practice active listening:** Engage in active listening exercises to hone your ability to fully understand others' perspectives and emotions during conflicts. Focus on being present, asking clarifying questions, and providing space for open dialogue.

2. **Cultivate perspective-taking:** Make a conscious effort to put yourself in others' shoes and consider their viewpoints, experiences, and needs. This helps

broaden your perspective and fosters empathy in conflict resolution.

3. **Strengthen emotional intelligence:** Enhance your emotional intelligence by developing self-awareness, regulating your emotions, and empathizing with the emotions of others. This allows for more effective management of emotions during conflicts.

4. **Seek feedback and learn from experiences:** Actively seek feedback from trusted individuals who can provide insights into your empathetic communication and conflict resolution skills. Reflect on past experiences, both successful and challenging, to identify areas for growth and improvement.

5. **Continuously learn and expand knowledge:** Invest in further learning about empathy, conflict resolution, and related topics. Read books, attend workshops or training programs, or seek out resources that deepen your understanding and provide new perspectives.

Remember, conflict resolution through empathy is a journey that requires ongoing practice and self-reflection. Be patient with yourself and embrace the opportunity for growth and development. By nurturing empathy in your conflict resolution efforts, you can contribute to creating more harmonious relationships, fostering understanding, and promoting positive change in your interactions with others.

7.7 CONCLUSION

As we conclude Chapter 7, we have explored the transformative potential of empathy in conflict resolution. Throughout this chapter, we have delved into the importance of active listening, perspective-taking, and emotional intelligence in fostering empathetic responses during conflicts. We have discovered that by embracing empathy, we can navigate conflicts with understanding, compassion, and the intention to find mutually beneficial resolutions.

Conflict is an inevitable part of our human experience, but it is how we approach and address conflicts that truly matters. Conflict resolution through empathy goes beyond surface-level compromises; it invites us to delve deeper into the emotions, needs, and perspectives underlying the conflict. By listening attentively, seeking to understand, and acknowledging the validity of others' experiences, we create a safe and supportive environment for dialogue.

Through empathy, we open doors to new possibilities and bridge the gaps that divide us. It allows us to recognize our shared humanity, despite our differences. When we choose empathy in conflict resolution, we choose to see conflicts as opportunities for growth, understanding, and connection.

Embracing empathy in conflict resolution also aligns with the teachings of Carl Rogers. It reflects his emphasis on acceptance, authenticity, and empathy as essential elements in human interactions. By practicing empathy, we honor the inherent worth and dignity of others, fostering an environment where conflicts can be transformed into catalysts for personal and relational development.

In this chapter, we have discussed the potential positive outcomes of conflict resolution through empathy, such as enhanced understanding, improved communication, strengthened relationships, collaborative solutions, increased emotional intelligence, reduced tension, and personal growth. We have also explored the potential pitfalls that may arise, reminding ourselves of the need for boundaries, self-care, and balanced power dynamics.

As we conclude this chapter, let us carry the principles of empathy into our daily lives. Let us continue to cultivate active listening, perspective-taking, and emotional intelligence in our interactions. By doing so, we contribute to a more compassionate and understanding world, one conflict at a time.

Conflict resolution through empathy is not always easy, but it is a worthwhile journey. As we move forward, let us embrace the challenges, learn from our experiences, and commit to continuous growth. By nurturing empathy in our conflict resolution efforts, we can create meaningful connections, foster understanding, and pave the way for transformative resolutions.

Thank you for joining us on this chapter, where we have explored the power of empathy in conflict resolution. May the lessons learned here inspire you to approach conflicts with empathy, compassion, and a genuine desire for resolution. As we move forward, let us remember that conflicts can be transformed into opportunities for growth, connection, and positive change when we choose to engage with empathy.

Chapter 8: Conclusion: Embracing the Teachings of Carl Rogers

Throughout this book, we have explored the profound teachings of Carl Rogers and their application in various aspects of our lives as leaders, individuals, and agents of change. From the art of active listening and creating psychological safety to understanding emotional intelligence, practicing perspective taking, nurturing a growth mindset, embracing authenticity and vulnerability, resolving conflicts through empathy, and cultivating unconditional positive regard, each chapter has unveiled valuable insights and practical strategies for personal and professional growth.

As we culminate our journey with Carl Rogers, it is essential to reflect on the cumulative wisdom we have gained and the transformative power it holds. The essence of Carl Rogers' teachings lies in the belief that genuine human connection, empathy, and acceptance can transcend barriers, foster growth, and facilitate personal transformation.

By integrating these teachings into our lives, we embark on a path of self-discovery, compassion, and authentic leadership. We recognize the inherent worth and dignity of every individual, valuing their unique perspectives and experiences. We understand that active listening, empathy, and emotional intelligence are not just skills but essential qualities that enrich our relationships, promote understanding, and create harmonious environments.

To practice the teachings of Carl Rogers is to commit ourselves to continuous growth, both individually and collectively. It means embracing vulnerability and being open to learning from our experiences. It requires us to challenge our own biases, embrace diverse viewpoints, and approach conflicts with empathy and a willingness to find collaborative solutions. By nurturing a growth mindset, we unlock our potential for personal and professional development, embracing challenges as opportunities for learning and growth.

Living the teachings of Carl Rogers empowers us to create psychologically safe spaces where individuals feel valued, heard, and supported. It encourages us to lead with authenticity, allowing our true selves to shine, and inspiring others to do the same. It fosters an environment where unconditional positive regard becomes the foundation for healthy relationships, empowering individuals to fully express themselves and reach their highest potential.

As we conclude this journey, let us remember that the teachings of Carl Rogers are not mere intellectual concepts but invitations to embody compassion, empathy, and understanding in our daily lives. Let us practice active listening, approach conflicts with empathy and curiosity, and nurture an environment of growth and acceptance.

By embracing the teachings of Carl Rogers, we become catalysts for positive change—leaders who inspire, empower, and create meaningful connections. The impact of our actions reaches beyond ourselves and extends to the individuals and communities we serve.

Let us carry the essence of Carl Rogers' teachings within us, becoming beacons of empathy, growth, and personal transformation. May we strive to create a world where acceptance, authenticity, and unconditional positive regard are the cornerstones of our interactions.

Thank you for embarking on this journey of self-discovery and growth. As you apply these teachings in your life, may you find fulfillment, forge deeper connections, and leave a lasting legacy of compassion and understanding.